Llewellyn's
2008
Witches'
Companion

An Almanac for Everyday Living

Spring 2008 to Spring 2009

Llewellyn's 2008 Witches' Companion

ISBN 978-0-7387-0560-6

Cover art © Tim Foley
Cover designer: Gavin Dayton Duffy
Designer: Joanna Willis
Editor: Sharon Leah

Interior illustrations: Neil Brigham: 199, 203, 205; Kyle Fite: 22, 25, 28, 75, 125, 129, 131, 211, 213, 216; Tim Foley: 9, 39, 43, 45, 63, 96, 103, 106, 121, 150, 153, 156, 159, 185; Tina Fong: 84, 113, 117, 170, 172; Lydia Hess: 33, 79, 90, 161, 163, 164, 166; Rik Olson: 11, 16, 18, 67, 69, 139, 141, 145, 220, 221, 222, 224, 225, 226, 228, 229, 230, 232, 233, 234; Carolyn Vibbert: 52, 56, 60, 176, 178, 187, 192, 195, 237, 240, 242

Additional clip art illustrations: Llewellyn Art Department

Any Internet references contained in this work are current at publication time, but the publisher cannot guarantee that a specific location will continue to be maintained.

You can order Llewellyn annuals and books from New Worlds, Llewellyn's magazine catalog. To request a free copy of the catalog, call toll-free 1-877-NEW-WRLD, or visit our Web site at http://subscriptions.llewellyn.com.

Printed in the United States of America.

Llewellyn Worldwide
Dept. 978-0-7387-0560-6
2143 Wooddale Drive
Woodbury, MN 55125-2989
www.llewellyn.com

Contents

Community Forum • 9

Provocative Opinions on Contemporary Issues

Witchcraft Essentials • 121

Practices, Rituals & Spells

Magical Transformations • 185

Everything Old Is New Again

The Lunar Calendar • 247

March 2008 to March 2009

Community Forum

Sink or Swim: Pagans and Mainstream Acceptance

Lupa

In November of 2006, a memorial plaque featuring a Wiccan pentacle was placed in the Northern Nevada Veterans Memorial Cemetery. It was in honor of Sgt. Patrick Stewart, who had died in combat in Afghanistan more than a year earlier. This would be the first victory in recent efforts to gain more official recognition of the Wiccan religion. Since then Wiccans and other pagans have participated in demonstrations and other civil rights campaigns using the momentum of that remarkable step forward. They have succeeded in convincing the U.S. Department

of Veterans Affairs to add the pentacle to a list of approved religious symbols for federal memorial markers.

These are just two of the more positive examples of the increase in media attention pagans, in general, have received in the past decade. While we still get daytime talk show hosts and nighttime reality TV shows exploiting us for higher ratings (and a few laughs), more serious examples of media coverage do exist. There are positive articles about pagans out there. And in the event of a not-so-good article, pagans are quick to respond in mature and polite letters (though there are still a few folks who let their emotions get the best of them!).

All this seems to mean the pagan community is heading toward mainstream acceptability. Granted, shows like *Wife Swap* and *Mad, Mad House* aren't exactly stellar examples of respectable media coverage. However, we are at an awkward stage in our social development as a community. We're moving from the "You're a what? Never heard of it," and "You're EVIL!" stage to the novelty stage. It looks as though in the next decade we may very well end up in the small, sometimes misunderstood, religion slot that the mainstream considers legitimate.

We do still have to deal with our growing pains. No doubt, both the community and individual pagans will experience a lot of bumps in the road before our general thinking about our religions matures. It looks like a reasonable bet that we're going to continue in this direction. But is that a completely good thing?

Out of the Counterculture

Paganism, at least in the U.S., really took hold during the 1960s and 1970s, at a time when people were rebelling against the shortcomings of the mainstream, speaking (and acting) out against racism, sexism, homophobia, environmental destruction, and even religious oppression. A cultural revolution occurred in which old standards were exchanged for new ones that many people perceived to be healthier.

It was the perfect time for paganism to take root. Goddess spirituality and a more eco-conscious focus on ritual and belief found a home in that "alternative-friendly" atmosphere. If someone didn't want to go to church, well, no problem. The counterculture allowed for all forms of religious expression, from liberal Christianity to Eastern religions, and yes, paganism. Pagans found a solid home outside the mainstream, and while there were probably some more conservative pagans both in and out of the closet, this particular time period infused the pagan community with a definite alternative bent overall.

It was this safe space for being "weird" that was one of the many reasons I embraced the pagan community, when I first became interested in pagan religious paths. I'm (gender) queer, kinky, and identify as otherkin, among other subculture interests. So it was nice to find a spiritual and social community that didn't ostracize me for not being entirely straight and vanilla (though there were certainly good folks of that persuasion as well). While I didn't become a pagan simply to avoid intolerance, I did join the pagan community in part because I was tired of being told I was sick, evil, and otherwise just wrong.

And who was telling me that? They were primarily Christian and overwhelmingly straight (either that, or extremely well closeted) in mostly Midwestern small towns or suburban areas where I grew up. Granted, growing up in the rural Midwest, I didn't have a lot of exposure to anything outside of the mainstream. I didn't watch much television, and I read the newspaper mainly for the comics. It was later that I discovered "Christian" didn't always mean conservative, that gays weren't tearing apart the moral fabric of the country, and that I wasn't the only person who saw nature as divine. For the first two decades of my life, though, I learned to associate the mainstream with bad things.

> **Like it or not, the media is one of the main forces in determining whether the general public will accept pagans, and that means pagans will be subjected to the biases of the general public.**

Today, I understand that the mainstream isn't entirely composed of bigots and other unpleasant people. It has a diversity all its own. Still, I worry about some disturbing trends that may end up infecting the pagan community as we become more acceptable. I don't think it'll come from outside, either—the biggest potential for trouble comes from within.

Preparing the Sacrifice

In recent years, I (and others) have observed a trend in the GLBT community as people have worked to reverse the tides of homophobia. Gays and lesbians have become more acceptable to mainstream society; and although the situation is far from perfect, there's been significant progress.

Still, this increased acceptance has come with a price. In recent years, internalized transphobia has become more common in the GLBT community, with gays and lesbians openly distancing themselves from transgendered people. This is often due to the fear that the latter group is negatively impacting the former's chances of political and social acceptance by the mainstream. In this way, certain gays and lesbians have become hypocrites, treating transgendered people to the same bigotry that they themselves point out in heterosexuals. (Never mind that many of the participants in the Stonewall riot that sparked the GLBT rights movement were transgendered!)

There's a lesson for the pagan community in this. In the decade and change that I've been a pagan, I have noticed an increase in the resistance to more "fringy" members of the pagan community, particularly as we've seen more progress toward mainstream acceptance. For example, a few years ago Wren's Nest, a popular online news source that features articles of interest to pagans, included a link to a story in a gay newspaper about pagans in the GLBT community. One example was "woman at the BDSM workshop wearing a pentacle." This one brief description garnered several indignant responses from pagans who read the article, including Rev. Styx, who complained, "My spirituality is not here to embrace and celebrate someone else's sexuality." (This reminds me of arguments in more liberal Christian churches in which a few conservative members left because the congregation supported GLBT people.) Another person, Steph, wrote that she didn't want non-pagans "making assumptions about my alleged sexual practices based on the wild postulations of BDSM Media Hounds who also happen to be pagan."

As a member of the otherkin community, and being quite open in the pagan community as well, I've seen some pretty closed-minded remarks about the former from the latter. Otherkin are people who identify in some (generally nonphysical) manner as "other than human." The stereotypical example of otherkin is someone who believes she or he's a dragon or elf reincarnated into a human body. While I won't deny that the otherkin community has its share of nuts and flakes, it does bother me when pagans pass off the entire concept as too weird. More than that, though, I know there are pagans out there who are terrified that I or someone else who happens to identify spiritually as an animal or mythical being just might make it appear as if that's a common belief among all pagans.

Showing Our Best Faces?

This brings home the crux of the argument: do we include more controversial people in the public image of paganism? As a community, we really don't have specific spokespagans. We do have authors and elders who are willing to speak up, but articles about paganism often feature interviews with not-so-big-name pagans, too. This means that the media can get quite an earful from a variety of people, all with different backgrounds and experiences. I haven't seen too many cases where the pagan was the one who made the community

look bad. Generally speaking, that's been primarily the work of un-scrupulous reporters and/or editors who were out to sensationalize their topic. The same goes for reality TV and daytime talk shows. No matter who you are, the people in charge are going to do their best to make you look like an utter fool.

Like it or not, the media is one of the main forces in determining whether the general public will accept pagans, and that means pagans will be subjected to the biases of the general public. Homophobia and transphobia, as well as misunderstandings about polyamory, BDSM, and other subcultures, are often a part of the judgment call.

There are vanilla, straight, monogamous pagans out there who dress like any suburban inhabitant and don't have a fringy bone in their bodies. However, it can't be denied that a significant part of the pagan community does still overlap with various subcultures. Take polyamory, for example. A recent article from Salon.com showed that 30 percent of the polyamorous people polled identified as pagans. And in my own study of the otherkin subculture, the majority of survey respondents were pagan; the percentage of pagans within that particular community is high enough that otherkin is sometimes (erroneously) thought to denote a pagan religion. Not all pagans may be a part of the subcultures, but it's obvious that many of the subcultures certainly like their pagans.

What this boils down to is that a lot of pagans are involved in subcultures that the mainstream isn't so crazy about. While some keep the various aspects of their lives separate, others see their lives as a seamless whole. Additionally, a person does not have to embrace something to show support (or disdain) for it. Otherwise, GLBT people wouldn't have had so many allies in Christian churches and other religious groups during their civil rights movement. If those allies had just said "I didn't become a (insert religious label here) to support what someone else does in the bedroom," the GLBT community would be in a much worse place today.

A Place at the Table for All

Chances are good that I have mentioned a subculture or two that you don't particularly agree with. You may think that transgendered people are just confused, or that otherkin are simply seeking attention. Yet keep in mind that many people in the mainstream still view pagans in the exact same way (and worse). Do you expect those

people to accept you and everything you believe without question? Or do you allow them room to agree to disagree, while not impeding the religious rights of pagans?

I see the same situation in play internally. You don't have to like members of a particular subculture that overlaps with paganism. However, the individual expression of so many diverse viewpoints has been part of the fabric of the pagan community. (That includes disagreement, by the way.) It's inevitable that not all of them will mesh.

However, I think it's incredibly important that we maintain the same level of diversity that we have since the community really got into swing nearly half a century ago. The freedom of individual expression is part of the weave of the fabric of the community; otherwise how could we get people of so many varied paths to share the same space?

We must also continue to accept members of the pagan community who do tend to blend into the mainstream. And as more pagans are raising families, we need to be sure that there are family-friendly events and resources. And we need to remain a safe space for those who choose to remain in their various closets, whether the broom closet or otherwise. After all, just because some of us are loud and proud doesn't mean we have the right to blow other peoples' covers.

Yes, I believe we should continue to fight for religious rights for pagan religions. I think we're on a roll here. But I also think that we stand to do a serious disservice to our own. We may not have a Stonewall in our heritage, but we do have a history of un-broom-closeted fringy people who weren't afraid to be "too weird" for the mainstream, and who set the stage for the advances that the community is making today. Let's make sure that in our quest for mainstream acceptance, that we don't sacrifice our own in the process.

REFERENCES

Books

Lupa (2007). A *Field Guide to Otherkin*. Stafford, UK: Immanion Press, p. 211.

Internet Resources

Americans United for Separation of Church and State (2007). "Bush Administration Agrees To Approve Wiccan Pentacle For Veteran Memorials." Retrieved July 16, 2007, from http://www.au.org/site/News2?abbr =pr&page=NewsArticle&id=9077&JServSessionIdr007=2tvm1x6wc4. app5b.

Anonymous (2007). "Transphobia." Retrieved July 16, 2007, from http:// en.wikipedia.org/wiki/Transphobia.

Rev. Styx (2003). "Paganism Is Not An Alternative Lifestyle!" Retrieved July 16, 2007. from http://www.witchvox.com/wren/wn_detail.html?id =7893&offset=15.

Robinson, Margaret (2003). "Bi-Witching." Retrieved July 16, 2007, from http://www.witchvox.com/wren/wn_detail.html?id=7893.

Langley, Liz (2007). "Whole Lotta Love." Retrieved July 16, 2007, from http://www.salon.com/mwt/feature/2007/06/14/polyamory/index _np.html.

Steph (2003). "Keep BDSM Out Of It!!!" Retrieved July 16, 2007, from http://www.witchvox.com/wren/wn_detail.html?id=7893&offset=30.

Whaley, Sean (2006). "Wiccan Memorial Plaque Installed at Veterans Cemetery." Retrieved July 16, 2007, from http://www.reviewjournal. com/lvrj_home/2006/Nov-21-Tue-2006/news/10964992.html.

Lupa *is a pagan and experimental magician living in Portland, Oregon, with her husband and fellow author, Taylor Ellwood. She is the author of* Fang and Fur, Blood and Bone: A Primal Guide to Animal Magic, A Field Guide to Otherkin, *and* Kink Magic: Sex Magic Beyond Vanilla *(cowritten with Taylor). She may be found online at http://www .thegreenwolf.com.*

Illustrations: Rik Olson

The Queen's Quarter of the Fourfold Goddess

Mama Donna Henes

My passionate devotion to the Goddess extends over more than thirty years even though I am not an advocate of the triple-goddess paradigm that embraces the Maiden, Mother, and Crone archetypes. That paradigm doesn't resonate with me because it belies what I believe to be the true nature of Nature. The triple goddess is widely understood by pagans to represent the complete cyclical wholeness of life. She who is three is likened to the moon—whose mutability she mirrors—the tides, and the seasons. And therein lies the rub.

After decades of researching, teaching, writing about, and producing what I call celestially auspicious occasions—the specially charged energy days that mark the cycles of the cosmos, the earth's seasons, and the multicultural ritual expressions that they inspire—I can state unequivocally that the moon has four quarters, not three. A life long lover of the moon, I'm in a constant state of lunar awareness, attending to the process of my life and living in conscious accordance with the cycle of its four phases. It has long troubled me that so many triple-goddess models leave out one element, direction, season, moon phase, and stage of life. I yearned for the full range of inspiration that can only be offered by an all-encompassing goddess of all four quarters.

For millennia, the three faces of the triple goddess have, in fact, reflected the stages of women's lives: the developing youthful maiden, the nurturing fertile mother, and the wise old crone. This ancient triple goddess does still correspond with the life expectancy and experience of most women in the Third World, who live pretty much as they always have. The reality of their existence dictates that they grow quickly through an abbreviated girlhood into early and prolonged maternity. If these women manage to survive multiple childbirths and general poverty, they pass through menopause directly into old age and death.

While there is still much to learn from the triple-goddess model, the old construct is not all-inclusive. This paradigm doesn't include a description of my life or the lives of other contemporary women in their middle years living in modern developed countries. It does not address our issues and needs, nor does it embrace our unique and unprecedented position in society. It does not even recognize our existence.

Contemporary Women in Midlife

We have outgrown our tenure as maidens and as mothers, yet old age no longer immediately follows menopause, which is why so many of us don't see ourselves (yet) as crones. There are now, for the first time, entire multinational generations of women for whom the triple-goddess paradigm no longer resonates. For nearly sixty million climacteric women in the U.S. alone, the Maiden-Mother-Crone ideal is flawed. So who are we supposed to be? And who can teach us how? Where is our authentic archetype?

We occupy a unique position. This extended and vigorous midlife period is largely unaccounted for in myth and archetype because such longevity has never before occurred for the great masses of women. We need a new body of accurate and empowering examples, role models, and teachers to encourage us as we explore the unfamiliar terrain of our changing lives and create new and joyful ways of being in charge of our own destiny.

Positive depictions of powerful middle-aged women are few and far between in folk tales and historical documents. There is no codified body of literature to which we can turn for affirmative illustrations of profound and potent midlife. The media has typically portrayed menopausal women as over-the-hill, overwrought flakes or furies who are completely undesirable. Real-life role models are sparse, although, in every society there have been notable and remarkable exceptions. Powerful middle-aged women who were rulers, adventurers, artists, entrepreneurs, scientists, spiritual leaders—and who also were glamorous and courageous.

Clearly, it is time for a new paradigm. Life is about change, which is, after all, the greatest teaching of the great cyclical Goddess. Her power and inspiration lies in her infinite flexibility, her adept adaptability, her unbounded ability to always, always, always change. The Goddess, supreme mistress of the art of transformation, will surely respond to the changes in our lives and times by enlarging the vision of herself to include her fourth dimension—and ours. The Goddess is, even now, beginning to expand to include us in her archetypal embrace.

Enter the Queen: A Fourfold Goddess

Given the absence of a traditional mythic example to spur me on and sustain me through my midlife changes, I desperately felt the need to invent one. So I formulated a fourth stage of development— the Queen—that would place my generational sisters and me after the Mother and before the Crone in a newly defined continuum of

womanhood. The Queen is a recognizable role model for our mature, masterful, and majestic middle years.

As I began integrating my concept of a fourfold goddess into my circles and workshops, women responded with an unexpected passion. Clearly, this enthusiastic reception speaks to the need we feel to find a divine model that truly represents our lives. I have always said that I practice my religion exactly the way my foremothers did fifty thousand years ago. I make it up as I go along. The fourfold-goddess model resonates with our particular circumstances and personal experience and serves as an authentic archetype for many women today.

My construct of the fourfold goddess—Maiden-Mother-Queen-Crone—is a much more accurate description of the four stages of a woman's life in the current way of womanhood. Her four periods of growth and transformation resonate deeply with contemporary women. They are in complete metaphoric alignment with the pervasive way that people have always ordered existence into four quarters: the four quarters of the moon, the four seasons of the year, the four solstices and equinoxes, the four elements, the four cardinal directions, and the four periods of the day.

As the model of the fourfold goddess took shape, I developed a new set of correspondences between her four stages and the four moon phases, the four seasons, four elements, four directions, and four daily periods that made metaphoric sense to me.

Fourfold Correspondences

Maiden	Mother	Queen	Crone
Waxing Moon	Full Moon	Waning Moon	Dark Moon
Spring	Summer	Autumn	Winter
Water	Earth	Fire	Air
East	South	West	North
Dawn	Noon	Sunset	Midnight

Is this hubris? Who am I to challenge an archetype that has been so powerful for so long? I am a proud member of the pioneering sixties generation, and consequently, I have a modest amount of experience in rebelling against the status quo of old archetypes and striving to replace them with new, more inclusive, and relevant ones.

Our generation has demonstrated time and again that it is possible to create our own characters, compose our own scripts, and author the sagas of our own lives. Bereft of affirming depictions of our lives, we women-of-a-certain-age are more than ready, willing, and capable of creating our own role models.

The fourfold goddess was born of my need and desire for a divine model whose conditions and changes mirrored my own. Her third aspect, the Queen, became an inspiring mythic mentor for me, representing and embracing, as the Goddess does, an emboldened, empowered, impassioned midlife. She came to exhibit a forceful persona of her own, impelling me through the maze of my troubled transformation. Though I conceived of her, in the end, she taught me. The clearer she became as a guiding archetype in my own life, the more I sensed her incipient presence in the lives of other women around me.

The mythic model I envision for the middle years of a woman's life is not yet old, but no longer young. The Queen stands in her proper place after the Mother and before the Crone—still active, sexy, and vital. She has the enthusiasm and energy of youth, and is tempered with the hard-earned experience and leavening attitudes of age.

By the time a woman reaches her midlife years, she has been forced to face and overcome obstacles and hard lessons, including her own shadow. Agitated with the unessential and restless for authenticity, she sheds attachment to the opinions of others and accepts responsibility and control for her own care, feeding, and fulfillment.

She is the queen of her self, the mature monarch, the sole sovereign of her own life and destiny. Here, finally, is an archetype that fits.

THE QUEEN OF HER SELF

The queen paradigm promotes a new understanding of what it might mean to be a middle-aged woman today—a woman who accepts responsibility for and to her self, and who celebrates the physical, emotional, and spiritual rewards of doing so. Becoming a queen is not automatic, nor is it instantaneous. As Simone de Beauvoir said, "One is not born a woman, one becomes one."

The Queen is the phoenix that rises from her trials by fire. She bursts forth from adversity and previous constraints, actual or imagined, to become a proficient player in the game plan of her choice. The Queen does not invite hard times and trouble, but she chooses to use them well.

Fully engaged, actualized, organized, efficient, self-sufficient, competent, ethical, and fair, the Queen has struggled for and earned her authority and respect. Determined and firmly centered on her own two feet, she dares to climb, step after step, with nascent surety into the heady realm of her own highest majesty.

Once on her throne and crowned, the Queen glows with confidence, competence, and grace. She is fully aroused and takes great pleasure in the feelings of freedom, elation, and wellbeing that come from personal empowerment. This thrilling post-menopausal period of vitality, renewed energy, enhanced self-esteem, optimism, and enthusiasm comes to us in direct proportion to the intensity of our own conscious, conscientious engagement in the process and consequences of transformation.

Another gift of self-enfranchisement is the potent and extremely liberating sexuality of the Queen. Shining from the inside out, her attractiveness and attraction is rooted deeply in her self-actualization, self-worth, and inner strength. She exudes a primal perfume of excitement, her power palpable in her very presence. Her desire reaches the boiling point and her inhibitions melt in the heat of her renewed passion for life.

It was through my own process of coming of age that I conceived of the Queen as the missing link in the chain of life for modern women in the heretofore incomplete triple-goddess archetype. Through my own intentions and concerted efforts, by constantly questioning, reevaluating, and reconfiguring, I reinvented myself in the image of the woman I had always hoped to be.

Through struggling to acknowledge, mourn, and then release what was irrevocably lost, I was able to recover my own misplaced vitality, interest, and energy after the long, hard, painful years of my disconcerting midlife changes and all of the hard knocks, bad news, and terrible truths that I had overcome in the fiery process.

My internal work eventually paid off. Completely self-realized for the first time in my life, I was ready, able, and actually willing to reign—to accept the responsibility for the truth and complete consequences of my own dreams, decisions, and actions.

I was a maturing monarch prepared to regulate all of the inner and outer realms of my own domain. I knew myself to be the uncontested mistress of my own fate. Miraculously, it seemed, I had succeeded in turning my midlife crisis into my diamond-encrusted crowning achievement. Surely, I was a queen, and not a crone. I was and am and intend forever to be the queen of me. The more I think about the Queen, the more I become her. And the more queenly I become, the more I desire to be in the company of other queens.

May every woman fulfill her goddess destiny and become the queen of her own life. And may all queens everywhere band together in our mature, centered power and focus our considerable sovereign skills on creating a sustainable, safe, and sane world for us all.

Long live the queens!

Mama Donna Henes *is an urban shaman, award-winning author, popular speaker, and workshop leader. She has published four books, a* CD, *and an acclaimed quarterly journal; and she writes a column for* UPI (United Press International) *Religion and Spirituality Forum. For the past thirty-five years, she has tracked and celebrated the cosmic cycles of the seasons, as well as the universal seasons of human life. Mama Donna's special concern is finding ways to reconnect the urban population with the wondrous workings of the natural world. To that end, she leads joyful celebrations of celestial events that have introduced ancient traditional rituals and contemporary ceremonies to millions of people in more than 100 cities since 1972. Mama Donna maintains a ceremonial center, spirit shop, and ritual practice; and she consults with individuals, groups, institutions, municipalities, and corporations to create meaningful ceremonies for every imaginable occasion. Mamma Donna Henes can be contracted through her Web site at http://www.thequeenofmyself.com.*

Illustrations: Kyle Fite

In Defense of the Maiden

Magnolia Clark

Young women—the Maidens—often get the impression that older women want to dismiss them. There are articles wherein older women writers say things like: "Our society must appreciate our beauty, it must finally see our worth and stop ogling all those thin young girls."

But shouldn't we appreciate the beauty of thin young girls and young women, and value them, too?

Signs of a subtle prejudice against the aspect of the Maiden can be found in books and magazines on the subject of women's spirituality, as well as in

It's time to put away old prejudices and misogyny, to let every woman be who and what she wants to be, and to go where her heart leads her.
MAGNOLIA CLARK

statements made by some older women who follow the goddess path. Instead of saying all women are important, the young woman is frequently put down, often ignored, or spoken of harshly because of the form of attention she receives in the media. Though, oftentimes, it is the media that tells us how we "ought to be."

Rather than criticizing the young women who appear in magazines and on TV, we could ask why the media thrives on showing scantily-clothed women. And isn't it a shame that young women are only honored in this way? We could fault our society—and the media—for focusing too much on the maidens while they ignore the mothers and crones.

When we follow the Goddess, we learn and understand that all women—regardless of background, mindset, or age—need to follow their own hearts . . .

When young women read such articles and hear such words, they may believe that they should be ashamed of being young, or that they don't really become worthwhile until they are older. It can seem, to the young woman, that older women are envious. And out of frustration, a young woman might do what she says she is against and speak harshly about the older women—the mothers and crones.

The Trinities Throughout History

In ancient times there were trinities such as the Fates, the Charities, and the three sides of Hecate. The Fates (Clotho, Atropos, and Lachesis) were the creators of destinies and lives. The Charities (Euphrosyne, Thalia, and Aglaia) represented grace, art, and inspiration. Hecate, goddess of power and sorcery, always has three bodies and three heads, all connected to one core.

There is something magnetic in the idea of a trinity—the three-in-one concept. Christians pay tribute to the Father, Son, and Holy Spirit; Hindus revere Shiva, Vishnu, and Brahma; and many contemporary woman identify with the trinity of Maiden, Mother, and Crone.

The Goddess Can Hold Everyone

The Maiden is the young woman who is full of curiosity and youthful exuberance. The Mother is mature and fertile, and she has a deeper understanding of life. And the Crone is the high priestess of knowledge, a woman who has lived a long life and gained bountiful wisdom. Because these three archetypes represent the three phases in a woman's existence, the unattractive, sagging older woman and the "dum-dum" young woman stereotypes are equally offensive.

The Maiden is as important as the Mother and Crone. So, rather than dismissing her, as many people do, we need to adore all the phases of womanhood. The ancient trinities still exist today because they show the importance of inclusion and acceptance—the different aspects coming together to make one.

The trinities are called their name for a reason—there are always three. Atropos and Lachesis would be incomplete without Clotho, just as the Charities could not work with only two goddesses. Hecate would be defective if a part of her were missing. The value of the trinities is found when they come together in their fullness. All three need one another. The mothers and the crones won't be revered while they're dismissive toward the maidens and vice versa.

A Renaissance of the Old Religion

Many people are drawn to a feminist-based spirituality because it acknowledges a woman's strength and power. It would not be fair to say other religions aren't for women; however, some religions have had leaders—usually well-known leaders—who have not been fair to women. Because of this, a lot of women want to make a new start with a new form of spirituality. This renaissance of the Old Religion stems from a faith that reveres women in all aspects of the goddess.

The idea that slender girls are beautiful won't vanish in a puff of smoke because it's too entrenched in our media and culture. But couldn't we use that as a spur to gain more acceptance for everyone. There's really no point in making young people feel their bodies are bad just because many have deemed it the only attractive body type.

We can work to gain more acceptance for other body types. We can add other feminine ideals of "beauty" to our current thinking. When we follow the Goddess, we learn and understand that all women—regardless of background, mindset, or age—need to follow their own hearts and minds. This is about inclusion, not exclusion. For women to be strong, they must rise together, and not create these petty clashes.

Magnolia Clark *is a writer in the symbolic Maiden phase of her life. She enjoys telling stories, researching history, reading, and drawing. One of her favorite pastimes is studying world religions and mythology, which she does to discover more about humanity and the world.*

Illustration: Lydia Hess

Granola Wicca: Religion for Fruits, Flakes, and Nuts

Elizabeth Barrette

Let's face it: there are some things about paganism that people think are silly—because they are silly. Even the most tolerant witch will sigh and roll their eyes, and then deny any association. Maybe it happens when you go to a festival and realize that person next to you is describing a personal path as light and flaky as trail mix. Maybe it's when you pick up a new magick book and exclaim, "Oh holy Thoth on a toadstool, somebody published this dreck?" These are some hallmarks of Granola

Wicca—that squirrelly branch of paganism inhabited by the fruits, nuts, and flakes among us.

Dramatis Personae

Many pagans are delightful folks. If you go to any kind of event, you will wind up meeting some of them. Even if you stay at home in your broom closet, you won't be able to avoid them altogether. You'll hear about them, read about them, occasionally stumble across one who somehow intuits your religion and strikes up a conversation. And then, well, there are the other ones, like . . .

The Goddess Incarnate (and Don't You Forget It)

She's often the first person a newcomer meets. She is the leader of her coven and always looking for new followers. She happily hands out pearls of wisdom. She can put on a spectacular ritual and manifest the Goddess in grand style. The problem is, she expects to be treated like a goddess all the time. Anyone who doesn't follow her script becomes the target of divine wrath, and while she won't tolerate challengers to her power within her own coven, she often gossips with her sisters who are also goddesses incarnate in their covens. What this means is that one misstep can get someone blacklisted all over the place.

The Hexmaster

This is a guy you don't want to piss off. He wears heavy jewelry with black stones. He has wands and staves decorated with animal skulls and strange crystals. His house is full of candles in garish shapes and colors that obviously didn't come from a supermarket. There are plaques with archaic engravings and downward-pointing pentagrams. And he tells these stories about all the people who have crossed him and how he got revenge. People listen because the stories are fascinating in a hair-raising kind of way, and because they are sometimes darkly hilarious. The hexmaster can often be found in the company of people who have just lost a job or gone through a messy divorce.

The High Priest/Priestess of Burnt Offerings

Everyone has things they can do and things they can't, but not everyone can tell the difference. In any large group of pagans, there always seems to be one with delusions of grandeur in the kitchen. This is the person who volunteers to bring fudge and delivers asphalt, who promises soufflé and sends explosions, who pledges fondue and produces a fire truck. Any self-respecting PTA member would know what to do, but somehow pagans tend to flounder. In the end, though, someone has to find a loving and empowering way to say: "Next sabbat, you bring the soda."

Drama Queen

Oh my goddess, it's an hour before the esbat and the ritual isn't finished! What if nobody comes? What if it's a total disaster? Every esbat, sabbat, and other coven activity you get a front-row seat to this show. And, at random times throughout the month, the Drama Queen of the witches calls everyone she knows to wail about the hardships of her love life, her work life, her school life, and every other crisis-of-the-day. Take what she says with a grain of salt—and some popcorn.

Pan's Man

He is a gift from the gods to women. He may offer to show you where he has that tattooed on his flesh. Or he may simply have it

all on display, if the site is clothing-optional. He can explain in great detail how all acts of love and pleasure are his rituals. Pan's Man can offer an instant introduction to all manner of erotic mysteries, or at least, to things that were mysteries before he started sharing them with all and sundry.

Bacchus's Babe

Like Pan's Man, she'll make love at the drop of a hat. Any hat (even a sun visor). This may be a great opportunity for single guys, but for married ones it can be a bit of a distraction. But hey, she's always got some of her boyfriend's home-brewed mead, or ale, or dandelion wine to ease the awkwardness. But watch out if she invites you back to her camp.

Often found together, Pan's Man and Bacchus's Babe make up a group collectively known as the party pagans. They enjoy drinking, smoking, and sex. They also like drumming and dancing the night away. Outside of their own kind, they do not work and play well with others as much as might be expected, given other people's unreasonable interest in sleeping after dark and in knowing precisely what they're about to put in their mouth. At a large enough site, they can be given their own camping area as a safe outlet for the wild life. (Enter at your own risk.)

Twitches

These are the young, exuberant newcomers to the Craft. Sometimes known as Twitches, these teen witches may form a coven of their own or join an existing one. They come in two flavors: light and dark. Light Twitches are perky creatures—full of questions and certain that the universe is a friendly place. Dark Twitches are moody, leather-clad shadows. Their view of the universe falls somewhere between tragedy and black comedy. Popular movies about witchcraft tend to set off surges of teen-witch activity.

Sabbat Pagans

Relatives of the Sunday Christians (often literally), these are people who practice their religion only on special occasions. It has little or no impact on their everyday lives. They can hide what they do so easily that some folks wonder why they do it at all. They may get along fine with mainstream folks and then have problems with those pagans whose religion intertwines with everything else in their lives. Not to mention that sabbat pagans are never around on the day after the sabbat to help clean up the mess.

Pompous Circumstances

Put three witches together and you get a ritual. Put three hundred together and you get a festival. Now multiply that times the number of nutcases in the pagan community, and you'll see why there are some rather weird stories going around about what happens at these events.

The Handfasting from Heck

It seems like a simple enough idea: take a little from the bride's religion, a little from the groom's religion, and create a matrimonial event that combines the best of both. But when one half is Wiccan and the other half is Christian, it can turn into cultural tug-of-war. Even two pagan traditions don't always mesh well, if one is Wicca and the other Asatru. While nobody may get burned at the stake, a handfasting may still turn into a horror story that the high priest(ess) will be telling for years to come. So if you get invited to an interfaith handfasting, you might want to check the location of the exits before you sit down.

"Womin" Space

Some womin come to Wicca because they feel that the Xian religion is all about men. They like to gather with other womin to celebrate "minstruation" and work magick. Like the hounds of Diana, these womin may pounce on any man who approaches their sacred rites, or their wominspace, and tear him to pieces. Other womin are gentle folks who protest against nuclear weapons, eating meat, and all other forms of violence. Some womin need to learn how to spell, and not the kind that involves a wand.

Men's Space

In the beginning, there was women's space. Then, some men decided that they needed a place where they could gather, worship the God, scratch where they itched, leave the seat up in the privy without getting screamed at, and not have to worry about stumbling into the wrong ritual where they might get torn to pieces. So men's space was made—usually at the far side of the festival site.

The Skyclad Ritual

In theory, worshipping in the buff is a pure and holy experience. In practice, it frequently turns into a pure and holy nightmare. On a cool night, you wind up edging closer and closer to the bonfire until your front bits are roasty-toasty and your backside feels ready to freeze off. On a warm night, you discover why the skyclad ritual is otherwise known as the Feast of Divine Flesh, which all good little mosquitoes dream about and hope to enjoy someday. Before long, the circle dance has devolved into a foot-stomping, back-slapping

caper of insect-slaying chaos accompanied by chants of "Better luck next life!" Following the release of circle, there is the obligatory mad dash for the house, then the ritual anointing with calamine lotion and the last chant: "Whose brilliant idea was this, anyway?"

THE ORGY

The orgy is that event everybody hears about but nobody ever really gets invited to. Along with the skyclad ritual, this is probably one of the main things that people point to in paganism as being "weird." People always like to talk about sex. Except, in this case, there isn't any. There are far more stories of orgies than there are genuine orgies. Just when you think you've tracked down an example, you discover that it wasn't really here, it was over there—not this Beltane, but last one—and your covenmate wasn't there, it was the covenmate's boyfriend's roommate. The truth scampers away faster than a nymph when a human bursts into the clearing, and the result is a similar letdown. Sadly, some folks seem to join Wicca with the hope of finding the mythical orgy. It's down that trail—right next to the fountain of youth.

Pagan Standard Time

This is the time at which the above events customarily begin. Note that, although Pagan Standard Time is often compared to Indian Standard Time, they are not the same. IST means "when everyone arrives." PST means "late," except on those occasions when it means "not at all." Experienced pagans are accustomed to this, but it can be very disconcerting to newcomers and curious onlookers.

Pagan History—or Not?

Once upon a time, pagan books were few and far between, mostly written by scholars, ceremonialists, and other folks who knew how to use footnotes. Then the floodgates opened. Today, there are hundreds of books on Wicca, magick, and historic (or not-so-historic) cultures. The resources used to create them are variable in quality and outcome.

Among the most famous examples of shaky scholarship is this statement: "Because they grew underground, potatoes were sacred to the Goddess and used in female fertility rites." What's wrong with the statement? The potato isn't native to Ireland; it was imported from South America by English explorers in the early 1500s. Placing it in the context of a "historical" Irish religion looks silly. It also resulted in new slang phases: "Potato trap" and "potato-goddess quotient" both refer to the presence of scholarly errors in a pagan book.

Another such example comes from a book on Druid magick. Referring to Atlantis, the author writes, "... when Atlantis disappeared ... many of its Sun-Priests washed ashore onto the Western banks of Wales— the one country most often referred to as the 'homestead of Druidism,' and there re-established ... their religion." Any reference to Atlantis as an origin undermines a historical claim, but there's more. Being Celts, the Druids migrated westward through Europe and appeared in several Celtic branches including Ireland, Britain, and Gaul. Later, in the same book, a carved pumpkin is listed as a symbol from "the closing era of Arthurian Britain." Like the potato, the pumpkin is an import; it originated in Central America, and spread from there through much of the Americas, but it was not introduced to Europe until sometime in the 1500s.

Furthermore, pagan authors may write about cultures without speaking the language(s) well, or at all. Attempts to write ritual components in an unfamiliar language often end in ludicrous failure. In his essay "The 21 Lessons of Hogwash," pagan scholar Isaac Bonewits provides a hilarious translation of the "Spell of Making" that goes, "Elements of Water which lead the god of rocks that mail hunger if knighthood your sapphire the great side of the axis as dark as the moon."

Pagans also have a tendency to chant nifty-sounding words or divine names without necessarily knowing the meaning. Through the centuries, people have read things in books and mispronounced words, or heard things at a festival and incorporated half-remembered bits into their own rituals. The result can turn into a gigantic game of "Telephone."

Not all the offenses are in conjunction with Celtic traditions, of course. The Celts are simply popular, and their historical record is patchy and sometimes contradictory. Errors creep in. It wouldn't be quite so bad if authors simply admitted to making things up. Not everything needs to be historical in order to be valid, after all. But when you claim to be relaying facts, and then get the facts wrong, it makes people point and snicker.

Truths and Consequences

If people don't want a witch to deliver the benediction before a meeting or other important occasion, it could be because they're plain old bigots. But it could also be because they've heard of the people described in Dramatis Personae. Or worse, they've met some of them. Too many pagans don't get along well with mainstream folks; and those who can, often can't get along with other pagans. Interactions between the groups can turn into a comedy of errors.

If newcomers to paganism decide to practice alone, maybe they're solitary by nature, or maybe they've attended some kind of Pompous Circumstance that was such a turn-off it pushed them away from group activities. True, many people come to paganism seeking an escape from stifling hierarchies. But let's not throw the baby out with the bathwater when it comes to organization.

According to Sturgeon's Law, 90 percent of everything is crud. Theodore Sturgeon, a science fiction writer, made his original remarks in response to attacks against science fiction books, but the sentiment may apply to books about magick and paganism as well. It doesn't excuse writers who hand in ludicrous manuscripts, editors who let them get away with it, or consumers who gleefully absorb the results. Once published, a dumb mistake can go on doing damage long into the future. When any field of publishing becomes clogged with errors, it earns a bad reputation that can also last long into the future. Academics, in particular, get their jollies by throwing rocks through the holes in other people's logic.

The Charge of the Goddess directs us to have "mirth and reverence." There's a delicate balance between being able to laugh at yourself and making a laughingstock of yourself. Part of pagan culture includes acknowledging the mix-ups and not trying to make excuses for the ridiculous. It's a reminder to not take ourselves too seriously, while we still search for solid foundations worthy of serious respect. Even the gods have their tricksters, because laughter leads to growth. So the next time something makes you shake your head and sigh, laugh it off, and look for the lesson in it.

Resources
Books and Articles

Adaire, Cairril. (2002). "Creating the Pagan Future: Professionalism." *PanGaia* #33.

Archer. (2004). "Bumps Along the Pagan Path," *PanGaia* #39.

Bonewits, Isaac. (2006). *Bonewits's Essential Guide to Druidism*. Seacaucus, NY: Citadel Press.

McCoy, Edain. (1993). *Witta: An Irish Pagan Tradition*. St. Paul, MN: Llewellyn Publications.

Monroe, Douglas. (1992). *The 21 Lessons of Merlyn: A Study in Druid Magic & Lore*. St. Paul, MN: Llewellyn Publications.

Robbins, Trina. (2001). *Eternally Bad: Goddesses with Attitude*. Newburyport, MA: Conari Press.

Internet Resources

Bonewits, Isaac. (2006). "21 Lessons of Hogwash," an excerpt from *Bonewits's Essential Guide to Druidism*. Retrieved on July 23, 2007, at http://www.neopagan.net/21-Lessons.html.

Darkhawk. "On Eclecticism, Syncretism, Multiple-Path, and other Combinatorics." Retrieved on July 23, 2007, from The Cauldron: A Pagan Forum at http://www.ecauldron.com/eclecticism.php.

Hautin-Mayer, Joanna. "When Is a Celt Not a Celt? An Irreverent Peek into Neopagan Views of History." Retrieved on July 23, 2007, at http://draeconin.com/database/whennotcelt.htm.

Moondrip , Lady Pixie. "Lady Pixie Moondrip's Guide to Craft Names." Retrieved on July 23, 2007, at http://www.bewitchingways.com/humor/name.htm.

"Pagan and Craft Humor" by various authors. Retrieved on July 23, 2007, at http://www.wicca.com/celtic/humor/humor0.htm.

Pagan Nation (2007). "Reading List: Introduction," by various authors. Retrieved on July 23, 2007, at http://pagannation.com/ubbthreads.php/ubb/showflat/Number/55173/page/0/fpart/2.

"Pagan Standard Time Clock," no author listed. Retrieved on July 23, 2007, from The Witches' Annual, Arcane Crafts at http://www.turoks.net/Cabana/PaganStandardTime.htm.

Serith, Ceisiwr. (2000). A review of *The 21 Lessons of Merlyn* by Douglas Monroe (Llewellyn, 1997). Retrieved on July 23, 2007, at http://www.digitalmedievalist.com/reviews/21.html.

Spangenberg, Lisa L. "What Advice Would You Give Neo Pagan Authors?" Retrieved on July 23, 2007, at http://www.digitalmedievalist.com/faqs/scholarship.html.

Steincamp, Cathar. "You Might Be Giving Pagans a Bad Name If . . ." Retrieved on July 23, 2007, at http://www.bewitchingways.com/humor/bad_name.htm.

Elizabeth Barrette *has been involved with the pagan community for more than twenty years. She serves as the managing editor of* PanGaia *(www.pangaia.com) and the Dean of Studies at the Grey School of Wizardry (www.greyschool.com). Her book* Composing Magic: How to Create Magical Spells, Rituals, Blessings, Chants, and Prayers *came out in 2007 (New Pages). Her other writing fields include speculative fiction and gender studies. Elizabeth lives in central Illinois, where she enjoys networking with pagans, including coffeehouse meetings and open sabbats, herbal landscaping, and gardening for wildlife. Visit her LiveJournal—The Wordsmith's Forge at: http://ysabetwordsmith.livejournal.com.*

Illustrations: Tim Foley

Who Decides That "It" Is Only a Phase?

Raven Digitalis

Those who have honestly dedicated their lives to unconventional ways grow up, but they may not change for anyone or anything other than themselves.
RAVEN DIGITALIS

"It's only a phase" is a common accusation uttered by people who don't understand pursuits such as occult spirituality, nontraditional medicine, alternative sexuality, subculture involvement, or anything else that deviates from the "norm." These highly subjective opinions tend to be justification for anothers' interest in what isn't readily accepted or recognized in Western culture.

At the same time, some people actually do approach such things with fleeting interests. To say such a person is "passing through a phase" is appropriate in some cases. Everyone's motivation for approaching alternative paths is unique. It's only natural that some will find their footing better, or easier, than others.

Some people find the journey on a magickal path is a perfect expression of their spirituality and follow it for life; for others, magick is just a fleeting interest or hobby. It is all dependant on the person and their individual reasons for delving into the magickal arts. One's approach to magick, and anything in life for that matter, ends up creating the outcome.

Discovering a Life Path

Aside from those who are born into magickal families, or who are exposed to esoteric religion in childhood, the majority of practitioners discover the Craft on their own accord. Some people are introduced to it by a friend or family member, or they stumble across a book or Web site on the topic by happenstance.

The same holds true for a number of witches and magicians who may identify with a subculture. Goth culture—a lifestyle I strongly identify with and will discuss a bit here—is a subculture. People tend to be attracted to goth culture, as well as many others, as a result of seeing someone's visual expression thereof, or from being exposed to music that characterizes the lifestyle.

For many, these discoveries serve as springboards from which the beliefs and practices for the rest of their lives begin to manifest. Upon researching or experiencing the magickal arts, many witches and magicians report a feeling of "coming home." Many people feel a renewed sense of freedom and self-empowerment when they discover paganism and occult spirituality. Just the same, many people experience a profound sensation of comfort and acceptance when delving deeper into alternative culture, and feel right at home with its music, art, and aesthetics.

Experiencing Youthful Rebellion

On the flip side, some people who approach things that are deemed "alternative" simply want to explore different ways of seeing themselves and the world, and use such explorations as stepping stones on their unique path of personal development. If this occurs, it's usually in a person's youth and is intertwined with one's natural teenage rebellion, which is itself a spiritual act of soul-searching, whether it's consciously recognized or not.

The "red hot" phase, identified by sociologist Roger Straus in 1976, describes the initial period of exuberance and enthusiasm that occurs when a person discovers a path they resonate with and, as a result of overexcitement, becomes extreme in their approach. This exalted identification with a certain ideology often manifests in forceful, over-the-top behavior. When experiencing the red hot phase, a person wants desperately to share their new insights and epiphanies with anyone who will listen, feeling as though this path is truthful and right for everyone, rather than just themselves in the moment.

I'm a prime example. I went through different phases in my youth. Before I discovered the Craft, and when I had only heard of the gothic subculture, I was wearing loads of pentacle jewelry, capes, cloaks, and smearing black makeup down my face. I would also burn and rip apart Bibles and leave the remnants on church grounds, which was something I thought was insanely clever, effective, and deviously anti-Christian. Today, I look down very harshly upon such actions.

Obviously, that behavior was not pagan, and it was certainly not goth. In truth, I was giving a bad name to those who have devoted their lives to those lifestyles. My motivation was to shock the masses and little more. It was a silly, passing, youthful phase, one that many people go through before they eventually uncover their self-identity. I sometimes wish I could tell my younger self what I've discovered. However, I realize that I needed to go through those phases in order to finally find the dedication to understand what my paths of interest are all about.

Searching for Religion

A couple years prior to my Bible-burning phase, around the age of thirteen, I had become interested in Christianity. It was the only spiritual path I knew. Unfortunately, I didn't understand a simple truth I now take for granted, which is that religion is not necessarily spiritual, nor is spirituality necessarily religious.

Even at that young age, I felt the Christian teachings I was exposed to were disconnected from the answers I needed. And a lot of behaviors and ideas were presented with only the words of others to back them—people who represented the religion were all too eager to point their fingers at outsiders.

Now, I know that many churches preach happiness and non-judgment, but the church I experienced at age thirteen definitely was not one of them.

I believe "true" Christianity (following in the footsteps of the Christ) is akin to Wicca, most notably in the realm of ethics and morality. I realize now that the Christianity I pursued at the time was not true Christianity, as the religion's original teachings of peace and equanimity were buried by judgment, condemnation, and egotism. It is unfortunate that scriptures are often misinterpreted, twisted, and manipulated to fit whatever idea a person wishes it to be. So much of Christianity does not represent the religion in the truest sense.

On the other hand, many pagans and magicians are irresponsible or misinformed, or they see spirituality as separate from their daily lives. Similarly, those beliefs and actions may present a negative image to people who honestly seek spiritual fulfillment and personal empowerment. An astounding number of people end up shifting between pagan paths, Christian paths, Eastern paths, and so on, never really satisfied with any spiritual system. This is an understandable occurrence that has a strong lesson in it, which is that most spiritual paths are the same in essence but have different methodologies. It's all about how we utilize them and where we let them take us. Every path also has its faults and there will always be some among the flocks who misrepresent the original intention it was founded on.

Dabbling in Magick

Many people come to witchcraft and other earth-based or occult spiritual systems without any real dedication to the studies. These dabblers soon find themselves dissatisfied with the beliefs and practices of the system, and some may wonder why they didn't feel connected to the divine after performing a spell or two. The truth is, it's not that simple. There's a lot more to the whole of the Craft, which has always been a personal system that speaks uniquely to each practitioner.

Dabblers come from every walk of life. Dabbling is not necessarily a bad thing, and odds are we all do this to some degree with something. For example, I'm not Hindu or Taoist, but I dabble in Hinduism and Taoism from time to time, identifying with certain elements. I'm not big into hippie culture, but sometimes I'll jam out to some Bob Marley. We live in an eclectic society, which means that we integrate bits and pieces of various paths into our own in order to better form our own individual path in life. I strongly believe that there are as many different religions as there are human beings walking the earth.

If a person admits to being a dabbler, it's best if they maintain awareness of and respect for the path(s) that interest them. Until someone becomes a dedicated adherent to a certain path, they're really journeying and experimenting in foreign territory for an uncertain period of time. Again, if this is approached honestly and with self-awareness, there's no problem. If dabbling is approached with a "red hot" attitude or air of superiority after simply experiencing a portion of a path, everyone who is involved may experience ill effects.

Just as I was passionate about my own personal anti-Christian viewpoint, I loved the word "witch" as an antithesis. By wearing my newly discovered black lipstick and eyeliner, however, I ended up portraying an inaccurate image of both lifestyles because I had not

been immersed in either of them for an extended period of time. With experience comes growth, and I, like many others, ended up settling in the trueness of each expression. I found deeper meanings than my originally skewed ideas about the lifestyles would have allowed.

It's quite often the element of magick that draws a person to the path of witchcraft and other related systems in the first place. This initial approach is more common amongst youths, whereas intentional spiritual searching is more common amongst adults.

Because many people begin by dabbling in the magickal elements of Wicca, neopaganism, and similar paths, the focus is quite often thaumaturgic, that is, the intention is often to control one's external world rather than transforming themselves internally. These people often want to make stuff happen. This is understandable, especially in a culture that stresses subordination and conformity. We want to take the power into our own hands and see the intended changes in ourselves and the environment; we want to witness the power of magick all around us.

It is unfortunate that some seek to practice magick without the balance that can only be found in ritualized practices with practical spiritual knowledge. It is easy to believe that immense power comes with magick, and it certainly can. But power associated with magick is only attainable with a balance of both wisdom and application.

Dabblers are usually concerned with love spells, money spells, and things of that nature. However, without a firm understanding of the ways in which the mind and the universe work, the repercussions are not always considered. When dabbling in magick for purposes of controlling one's external reality, ethics and spirituality can often take the back seat to an unquenchable desire for self-assurance.

Fortunately, for all of us, the person who starts with a selfish approach will seriously connect to their path on a spiritual level, too. Influential power cannot be controlled or harnessed properly without a base of spiritual knowledge.

A License to Depart?

If magickal spirituality is so incredibly fulfilling for some people, why do others flee from such things as quickly as they came in? To expound on what I mentioned earlier, some people enter the Craft because they're searching for power rather than empowerment. When that externally influential power isn't discovered (sorry, no telekinesis), they leave the Craft behind, abnegating any spiritual benefit it could have provided. In a sense, this is a good thing because people who want abilities to dominate become discontented with the Craft when it doesn't provide that power. This is because true power comes from within, and personal magick isn't effective until the self is examined.

It's also true that some who do approach the Craft with spiritual intentions also leave unfulfilled. Everyone's experience in magick is different. Whereas some individuals may get exposed to deeply spiritual elements of magickal spirituality, others may find themselves exposed to empty rituals, gossiping peers, sexual predators, or elitist communities. Neither side of the coin portrays the full spectrum of the path; both exist, and both must be made aware of. At the same time, we all attract experiences into our lives that we must both come to terms with and learn from. While some magickal circles may not maintain spiritual "purity"—regardless of how "pure" the originator's intentions were—it's essential for explorers to have perspective, to learn from situations, and then move on to what better suits them.

Witchery and gothism are not lifestyle choices one just "grows out of . . . "

Personally, I think a lack of mysticism pushes people away from magickal spirituality. Mysticism can be defined as a quest seeking direct and personal communion with the divine. Necessarily mystical paths include Qabalism, Kabbalism, Merkabah, Sufism, and Esoteric Christianity. All of these paths are offshoots of an originary tradition, and all have been maligned to some measure by their progenitor. Considering modern Hermeticism's ties to Qabalism in particular, as well as Wicca's ties to indigenous or tribal-shamanic spirituality, modern magick, as a whole, is naturally connected to the mystical current. As the Charge of the Goddess says:

If thou findest not within thee,
then thou shalt never find it without thee.

The mystical experience makes our ideas and philosophies come alive. During the moments in which we merge our own consciousness with the Ultimate, we truly discover our own power. I believe if this mystical connection—this gnosis—is not experienced, then regardless of religion or spiritual path, a person's excitement and enjoyment of the path dissipates. Luckily, mysticism and spirituality transcend the parameters of religion.

Quite a few people will continue to experiment with magickal lifestyles and move on, fluctuating in and out of spirituality, not really adhering to the fullness of what any particular path has to offer. Magickal paths are, in the end, all about being yourself and discovering how to live your full potential. That's what makes these paths so solid and real. A great number of people who have not found their true callings get involved in magickal spirituality because it seems cool at the time, and actually miss the point of the lifestyle entirely.

Magickal paths provide a place for everyone to fit in to a much greater degree than mainstream society in general. But if magickal ways aren't approached with respect, intelligence, and honest self-seeking, the person who is interested will become little more than a drifter. I believe it is essential to research a wide variety of spiritual practices and learn as much as is feasible in as many areas as possible.

Growing Up

Many critics view alternative subcultures and the magickal path in a similar light, believing, for example, that because someone appears different, they are delinquent, juvenile, and childish—especially if they're past the teenage years. If that expression continues as the person grows older, they can be misjudged as clinging to

the foolishness of a pubescent phase that is marked by dressing up and being "alternative."

The thing is, it's not just a phase for everyone. Witchery and gothism are not lifestyle choices one just "grows out of," only to wake up and realize that conformity is best and that experimenting in alternative lifestyles was foolish in the first place. It's easy for people to misunderstand and believe we'll all grow up and go along with the accepted social-political flow one day; and if we don't, then it's our own stubbornness that is keeping us from conforming.

This view is typically a generational one. Most young adults today would disagree with that concept. Nevertheless, it's a view that people of alternative lifestyles must face. What one person might realize as a lifestyle choice others will wrongly critique as a phase.

Those who have honestly dedicated their lives to unconventional ways grow up, but they may not change for anyone or anything other than themselves. It isn't necessary to get married, have kids, buy a million-dollar home, or hold or a nine-to-five job. Certainly, it would be silly not to conform to some degree in this society, if for no other reason than to survive financially. The level of necessary conformity, however, is different for everyone. Fortunately, we are afforded much more freedom of expression today than in times past.

Everyone's level of personal dedication and soul-searching within each lifestyle varies and this results in a wide array of internal viewpoints. Thus, some individuals who become interested in these alternative lifestyles eventually come to realize that the philosophies, practices, and aesthetics don't speak to them at the core of their being. On the other hand, a number of individuals feel just the opposite and remain strong adherents to the lifestyle(s) for the rest of their lives.

I encourage every reader to examine their own motivations for pursuing the ways of magickal spirituality. Perhaps it would be a good idea to make a list of the pros and cons of your decided spiritual path, and meditatively reflect on where you find yourself in terms of your studies and practices. How did you first become involved in witchcraft and magick? What were your original motivating factors for pursuing that path, and where do you find yourself now? Where do you see the future taking you in terms of your spiritual studies and practices? What, in your life, do you believe is a phase of sorts, and what feels more permanent? What aspects of your magickal spirituality do you feel a calling to explore more deeply, and what aspects can you do without? Our individualistic viewpoints, experiences, and discoveries are what truly determine the magick.

Raven Digitalis *is the author of* Goth Craft: The Magickal Side of Dark Culture (Llewellyn, 2007), *and the forthcoming* Shadow Magick Compendium (Llewellyn, September 2008). *He is a fourth-year neopagan priest, cofounder of the "disciplined eclectic" shadow magick tradition Opus Aima Obscuræ, as well as a radio and club DJ of Gothic, EBM, and industrial music. With his priestess Estha, Raven holds community gatherings, tarot readings, and a variety of ritual services. From their home in Missoula, Montana, the two also operate the metaphysical business Twigs and Brews, specializing in magickal and medicinal bath salts, herbal blends, essential oils, and incenses. Raven holds a degree in anthropology from the University of Montana. He's also an animal rights activist and black-and-white photographic artist. Raven's Web sites can be found at www .ravendigitalis.com or www.myspace.com/oakraven.*

Illustrations: Carolyn Vibbert

Witchy Living

Day-by-Day Witchcraft

The Zen Pagan Path

Sandra Kynes

Many of us enjoy yoga for fitness; however, if you delve deeper into yogic practices, you become aware of subtle changes occurring in your body and in the way you approach life. You come to the core purposes of yoga, which are to prepare for meditation and to grow spiritually.

When someone feels and understands the real purpose of yoga, there are a couple of possible reactions: run for cover and remain committed to personal beliefs, or explore Eastern philosophies, like Buddhism and/or Hinduism. The latter's rich pantheon of deities have already filtered into pagan circles, and are, therefore, familiar to us. Actually, yoga began during the Vedic period of India's history around 3000 BCE, pre-dating Buddhism and classical Hinduism.

The yoga mat was a lonely place for the first several years as I tried to reconcile this Eastern practice with my Western paganism. I suppose it would have been easier to accept yoga as simply an activity that felt good and was good for me, but I have never been one to take the easy road. If there's a hard way to do something, that's usually how I do it. Seriously, though, as the spiritual person I am, I couldn't help but feel the pull of the yogic path, and just doing the *asanas* (postures) wasn't enough for me. Eastern practices are extensive and well documented, which brought me to the conclusion that they might provide some kind of guidepost or at least a new perspective on my chosen path.

The *Yoga Sutras of Patanjali*, is a compilation of ancient teachings that Patanjali, a great Indian sage, wrote down around 200 C.E. The *sutras* (short verses) are chanted. As I studied the sutras during the course of yoga teacher training, my instructor said something that made me go "Hmmm." He told us the sutras did not prescribe *what* to believe, but *how* to believe, and that the sutras actually validate all paths and religions. The most important tenets are integrity and true devotion. And so I came to realize that I could bring my spiritual beliefs with me to the yoga mat and go from there.

Another important thing I learned was that in the Vedic Golden Age, when yoga began, poetry was composed in honor of the forces of nature. This resonated with me. As a pagan, I honor and connect with the energy of the natural world through the use of ritual. The ancient yogis believed that the purpose of life was to experience *prana* (energy) flowing through all aspects of ourselves. In order to receive this flow of universal energy, we need to be in the moment, and it is through spiritual practices that we can create the space we need to be present and open to receive.

Yoga seemed less and less a separate part of my life and became another way to access energy; plus, it was providing a new in-road to my spirituality. My time spent on the yoga mat blossomed into spiritual time that I have come to cherish. In front of my altar and accompanied by the familiar Celtic pantheon, my practice of yoga evolved, but not into a tit-for-tat pagan version of it. I felt that by tapping into the energy and essence each posture embodied, I could gain a more subtle awareness and insight about my beliefs as well as the rich tapestry of myth that is woven into the fabric of paganism from the land of my ancestors. After all, myths weren't created for entertainment; they personify powerful archetypes and convey meaningful lessons. According to Jean Markale, the word *myth* originally meant "sacred story."

The three warrior asanas didn't conjure up images of Cúchulainn or Fionn Mac Cumhaill for me. Instead, it was the commitment and determination of these mythical characters that came to mind. What did it mean to be a warrior? Certainly not the shoot-em-up blood and glory stuff of Hollywood. I came to understand that being a warrior is about readiness, strength, and the courage to stand up for what is right. It is about protecting those who cannot stand up for themselves. In addition, and strange as it may seem, a warrior embodies non-aggression.

In all three warrior postures (especially warrior II), the chest area is wide open. Above all else, the warrior is compassionate—energy from the heart flows out to the world. The warrior works through peaceful means and not by the sword, unless absolutely necessary. Being a warrior is about truth and service. Celtic hero Cúchulainn's name, which means "the hound of Chulainn," gives a hint of this. Sétanta took this as his name as well as his life's purpose of serving

others. In the Druidic path I follow, service is an important component of life; it's an active form of truth and sharing of one's own energy.

Through the warrior postures I try to access the spirit and energy of strength and commitment for purposes beyond self and personal gain. In order to do this, it is necessary to quiet my chattering "monkey" brain that jumps from one thing to another, and gently guide my thoughts beyond everyday concerns. Rather than letting the mind wander to think, "Gee, I never noticed that muscle before," or "What am I going to eat after class," focusing the mind while holding a posture can be a challenge. It can also be a rich learning experience. Yoga truly becomes a unifying force for body, mind, and spirit—a harmonizing of personal energy.

B.K.S. Iyengar, who was instrumental in bringing yoga to the West, noted that the study of the self is one of the cornerstones of yoga. The Druid Greywind says that to know self allows you to know your true potential. Eastern and Western sages are saying very much the same thing: We need to find out who we truly are.

Getting to know more about myself and defining who I am (to myself) has brought me closer to the core of my beliefs. I always knew my spirituality was a major part of who I am, but I began to sense this on a different level. I found that moving inward was not a static experience and that over time our lives can become like a Mö-bius strip—a circle created by a strip of paper, metal, or whatever, that has been twisted once before the ends are joined so that the inner surface flows onto the outer surface and vice versa.

Like a Möbius strip, in meditation we move inward but eventually connect to the world outside ourselves. In time, we may feel the presence of the Divine in both our inner and outer worlds. As a pagan, I have always thought of the Divine in terms of a great goddess and felt more at home with yoga the more I learned about the people of India. In Celtic as well as Indian (Vedic and Hindu) cultures, the Goddess is fully immanent. In an ancient text called The Devi Gita (Song of the Goddess), the Mother Goddess advises people about the practice of meditation for self-knowledge.

While there are forms of meditation that require emptying the mind to rest in the grace of silence, most of us need a paddle to steer our canoe of chattering monkeys. Meditation has been likened to the flow of water in a river because it is a continuous flow of perception—a thought wave. Staying focused on this flow leads to realizations and truths. Like my perception of the warrior, it leads from outer to inner worlds and to the deeply personal. A room full of people

can start with the same thought—the meaning of being a warrior—and in the end there will be a room full of different results because each person's thought wave will be unique. Also, from day to day our own thought waves vary because we are not the same each day; time and energy are fluid.

Paramahansa Yogananda, founder of the Self-Realization Fellowship, brought Eastern teachings to the U.S. in the 1920s. Yogananda said that the state of meditation was active calmness (sleep was passive calmness). Modern yoga master Erich Schiffmann likens this state of stillness to a spinning top: while it may appear motionless, it is actually going full speed—and it is perfectly centered. In meditation and while holding a yoga posture, we come into that kind of active stillness following our thought wave.

Perhaps because I have practiced my faith mainly as a solitary, it was relatively easy for me to explore a circuitous path through the proverbial Druidic woods. As a result of these experiences many of my rituals have become more "quiet." Someone who observed me might say that I'm just sitting there meditating and not recognize that I am engaging in ritual, but I'm actually in that state of active stillness. In this state we are able to sense the natural world around us, to feel the pull of the moon, the turning of the seasons, and the presence of divine energy. Through this, we continue to explore who we are and what life is about.

The search for self transcends cultural boundaries and time. "Who am I?" and "What is life?" are age-old questions. The answers evolve as we grow. So exploring and re-exploring is an ongoing quest that takes us to new and different levels to find our deeper selves. We come to understand that we are embodied spirits and that being alive in these physical bodies allows us to become aware of our true nature while we are in nature.

Each time I return to mundane activities after yoga, meditation, or ritual, I bring a bit of that deep experience with me. It's an affirmation that my life continues to be a Möbius strip, integrating all the parts of who I am. From yogic practices to everyday life, active stillness becomes movement; intention is manifested as I hold my strands in the web of life. I have found yoga to be a powerful tool for self exploration and empowerment, and I no longer feel that dichotomy of cultures.

In the introduction to one of his books, Peter Berresford Ellis points out the linguistic relationship, parallels in ancient books of law, and other similarities as well as possible origins between Irish/Celtic and Indian/Hindu cultures. I would like to think that one of my very distant Irish ancestors may have also practiced some form of yoga.

References

Brown, Mackenzie C. (1998). *The Devi Gita*. Albany, NY: State University of New York Press.

Ellis, Peter B. (1999). *The Chronicles of the Celts*. New York, NY: Carroll & Graff Publishers.

Greywind. (2001). *The Voice Within the Wind*. Girvan, Scotland: Grey House in the Woods.

Lidell, Lucy. (1983). *The Sivananda Companion to Yoga*. New York, NY: Simon & Schuster, Inc.

Markale, Jean. (1993). *The Celts*. Rochester, VT: Inner Traditions.

Migdow, Jeff. (2000). *Prana Yoga Teacher Training Manual*. New York, NY: The New York Open Center.

Mira, Silva & Mehta, Shyam. (1995). *Yoga the Iyengar Way*. New York, NY: Alfred A. Knopf.

Schiffmann, Erich. (1996). *Yoga: The Spirit & Practice of Moving into Stillness*. New York, NY: Pocket Books.

Yogananda, Paramahansa. (1999). *Inner Peace*. Los Angeles, CA: Self-Realization Fellowship.

Sandra Kynes *describes herself as an explorer of Celtic history, myth, and magic, and is a member of the Order of Bards, Ovates, and Druids. She is a certified yoga instructor, massage therapist, and reiki practitioner; as well as an energy keeper and member of the Labyrinth Society. In addition to authoring four books, her writing, under the name Sedwyn, has appeared in several editions of Llewellyn's* Magical Almanac, Witches' Spell-a-Day Almanac, *and the* Witches' Calendar.

Illustrations: Rik Olson

Choosing to Be Vegetarian

Abel R. Gomez

Witchcraft is a path to mindfulness. As we develop our magickal practice and celebrate the cycles of Mother Earth, we learn that we are intimately connected to every being in the universe. Each of us is a strand on the vast web of life, and our ethics are framed with the knowledge that the choices we make have far-reaching effects. Some witches get involved in animal protection groups and ecological projects because they hope to cultivate a sustainable and compassionate future. As witches, most of us try to walk lightly on the earth and follow a path of awareness, knowing that our every action leads to the healing and spiritual progression of all beings. For many, this is particularly relevant in regard to food.

Many contemporary witches are vegetarian (they consume no animal flesh) or vegan (they do not consume or use any animal products, including diary and leather). Others believe that it is necessary for humans to consume meat and they choose to work toward more compassionate methods of raising livestock. Still, many witches and occultists are dismayed by the horrendous treatment of animals on factory farms and the ecological devastation that results. They feel that the vegetarian movement has relevance. It is a personal choice, but many believe it promotes both a compassionate and spiritually conducive lifestyle. Additionally, vegetarian and vegan diets are healthy, when properly planned; and they have been proven to lower cholesterol, reduce excess body weight, and even reverse heart disease.

As practitioners of a nature-based spirituality, witches understand that some creatures must die in order for others to survive. Many witches believe that compassion is at the heart of all real magick and that we should not shed the blood of the innocent, particularly when it is unnecessary. We hold that divinity shines through all beings and choose to abstain from meat, dairy, and eggs in an effort to live in harmony with all beings.

The practice of vegetarianism may be particularly relevant to modern witches in regard to occult progression. Great thinkers and philosophers such as Plato, Leonardo da Vinci, and Albert Einstein embraced vegetarianism and taught that it is an essential component to maintaining a healthy and compassionate world. Other thinkers, such as the Greek philosopher and mystic Pythagoras, taught that a vegetarian diet is essential to creating and manifesting inner peace.

Most of the spiritual dynamics of vegetarianism held by modern witches come from the spiritual traditions of the East. Eastern spirituality, like the concept of karma, reincarnation, and the chakra system, have had an enormous impact on contemporary witchcraft. Many sects of Buddhism, most notably the Mahayana tradition, prohibit the consumption of meat as a form of respect toward all beings. In many schools of Buddhist thought, it is also taught that meat is toxic for the body and soul, and to maintain a healthy lifestyle, one must practice non-attachment to that which is destructive.

Perhaps the most relevant spiritual implication of vegetarianism in modern witchcraft and occultism is in regard to energetic well-being.

The links to vegetarianism and spirituality are even more present within Hindu spiritual traditions. Most forms of Hinduism encourage adherents to adopt a vegetarian diet not only to show respect to other beings but because of the belief in immanent divinity. Like many contemporary witches, Hindus believe in manifest divinity, that is, that the divine shines through all beings. From this realization came the Eastern concept of *Ahimsa* (non-violence) toward all beings. Thus, many Hindus see eating meat as "sinful," in that it causes unnecessary suffering to other beings that are manifestations of the Divine. Though there are also a wide range of opinions on diet, the majority of Hindu scholars and saints believe that vegetarianism is essential to health on both a physical and a metaphysical level.

There is another component to vegetarianism in Hinduism, and that is in regard to karma. As witches, we recognize that every action there is a reaction. It is a law of physics. We also recognize

that what goes around comes around and that what we do to others will eventually come back to us. It has been said that a truly enlightened being does not interfere with the karmic path of another. This is true for Hindus and witches alike when it comes to the unnecessary slaughter of animals. Reincarnation also plays into this belief as we wish to show mercy to the animals we may one day become.

Today's witches may also notice the ascetic properties of vegetarianism. Vegetarianism and other dietary restrictions are practiced in spiritual traditions around the world in an effort to cultivate spiritual balance and awareness. Members of the Christian Orthodox Church, for example, follow a vegan diet during the forty days of

Lent and observe other fasts throughout the year in order to create clean bodies with which to focus on God. This concept is also present in a number of Christian traditions. Seventh Day Adventists, for example, advocate vegetarianism as a means of cleansing the body —the temple—of harmful and unclean substances.

Perhaps the most relevant spiritual implication of vegetarianism in modern witchcraft and occultism is in regard to energetic well-being. We recognize that all things have energy, a vibration that affects the aura and energetic bodies. The reason protection charms can be particularly powerful when kept close to the body is because they affect the aura. This concept can also be demonstrated in crystal healing as each stone has a particular energy that can bring healing. In both systems there is a recognition that mind, body, and spirit are connected. What is done to one part also affects the other two.

Similarly, many modern witches believe that, when we consume meat, we absorb the energetic qualities of that flesh into our bodies. Meat cannot be obtained without pain and suffering, and when we consume such products of slaughter, we ingest these energies into our bodies. This can have a number of psychological and spiritual ramifications that block psychic awareness and spiritual progression. It is also important because, as mentioned earlier, all things are connected, and the actions we take and the energies we produce also affect everything else in the universe.

Many occult groups and contemporary witches accept the above beliefs to some degree and suggest abstaining from meat before and during ritual and spellcraft.

Similarly, many schools of reiki suggest maintaining a vegetarian diet during a reiki attunement (energy initiations), to more easily facilitate energy flow. It has also been rumored that the priesthood of Avalon practiced vegetarianism to produce a deeper awareness of magickal forces.

For witches open to new possibilities, vegetarianism can be a path of compassion and expanded consciousness. It is an everyday commitment to living in harmony with other life forms in nature, and aligning oneself with reverence and respect to Mother Earth. Though it may not be for everyone, vegetarianism can be a revolutionary way to transform of one's view of the world. It can help us see all beings, not as utilities, but as allies and neighbors of the earth. Many witches have embraced vegetarianism as a life path, for as The Charge of the Goddess states: "My Law is love unto all beings."

Abel R. Gomez *lives in the California Bay Area. He is an actor and writer with a deep interest in myth, ritual, and symbolism of global spiritual traditions. His work has appeared in a number of neopagan publications, most notably* Copper-Moon, *an online magazine for young adult witches. He can often be found recycling, saving animals, exploring esoteric subjects, or doing the Time Warp.*

Illustrations: Kyle Fite

Simple Blessings

Susan "Moonwriter" Peznecker

Blessed Mother,
your child speaks.
You give me food that I
may never hunger.
I am grateful.
Blessed be.

Nothing connects us closer to Gaia than preparing and eating food. Food is one of earth's gifts to us—it keeps us alive and provides tangible awareness of earth's magickal bounty. Most of us eat or drink several times daily, each meal presenting a joyful opportunity for ritual and thankful awareness.

If food is a sacred gift from Mother Earth, it makes sense to prepare oneself before eating. The simple act of hand washing before a meal shows one's readiness to receive earth's beneficence. The use of a special soap—frankincense is

excellent for purification—adds to the magickal intent. Rinsing the hands with water poured from a dedicated ritual vessel or chalice can also become part of the cleansing ritual.

Creating an elegant, aesthetic setting is another way to echo the sacred importance of mealtimes. If a meal can be thought of as ritual, then your table is an altar space. Honor this by eating at the dining or kitchen table—rather than in front of the television or in your car on the way to work. Adorn your table with favorite dishes, seasonal linens, and fresh napkins, as befitting the food's importance. Add a candle, saltcellar, and a glass of fresh water to pull the elements into the setting and support the feeling of meal-as-ritual.

Offering a blessing is a wonderful way to bring one's meal into the sacred realm. The word *blessing* comes from roots meaning "worship" and "bliss." A blessing over food is a short piece of inspired writing that channels or contacts the Divine and invokes thanks, acknowledgement, or gratitude. You might begin by addressing a specific patron or deity, or you may choose a simpler, more universal blessing. Your thanks might be informal—spoken spontaneously, and in your own words—or could take the form of structured verse or ritualized words designed to be reused from day to day.

> *As this food is given me,*
> *Nature's blessings shall I see.*

If you're uncomfortable with spontaneity but don't care for structure, the words "thank you for this food" (or even just "thank you") are always appropriate. For a longer or more serious blessing, you might identify yourself and state your intention. Give the blessing and finish with signal words to show conclusion, e.g., "So mote it be" or "Bright blessings."

> *Blessed Mother, your child speaks.*
> *You give me food that I may never hunger.*
> *I am grateful.*
> *Blessed be.*

When offering the blessing, meditate on your intention, allowing spirit to fill and empower the words. Add to the mini-ritual by invoking the elements: light the candle, touch a fingertip-full of salt to your tongue, and take a sip of water before uttering the blessing itself. As you eat, be mindful of the food's nourishing qualities and the joy of eating something life-sustaining and delicious.

Once you've developed a blessing ritual that fits your needs, use it each time you take food or drink. Establishing this simple routine will increase your appreciation of nature's blessings, while bringing magick more surely into your daily life.

Susan "Moonwriter" Pesznecker *is a hearth pagan and a child of the natural world in all of its magickal guises. Conceived at Beltane, her magickal roots include the vampire lore of a family living in Europe's Carpathian Mountains, a Czech grandmother schooled in leechcraft, the Wicca and Pictish traditions of the highland Scots, and Nez Perce medicine ways. First trained as a nurse, Susan holds a master's degree in nonfiction writing and today works as a college writing teacher. Areas of magickal expertise include astronomy, green magick, herbology, healing, stonework, nature study, and folklore. For the last three years, she has taught magick at the online Grey School of Wizardry. As a fourth generation pioneer Oregonian, Susan is an aficionado of the art and rock art of Northwest Coastal and Columbia plateau First People. She loves to read, camp, and work in her organic garden, and makes her home in Milwaukie, Oregon.*

Illustration: Lydia Hess

Night of the Wolf

Susan "Moonwriter" Peznecker

I'll always remember the night we saw the wolf.

On the heels of a difficult workweek, we loaded the car and headed south for a weekend on Oregon's high desert.

Crossing Mt. Hood, the night was black and cold, and the road slick. Bill drove, maneuvering the car through the icy spots. We'd just passed the Bear Springs turnoff when we rounded a corner and saw, beside the road, a huge timber wolf. He stood just off the shoulder, watching us, following us as we drove by, his silvery coat glowing in the full moonlight.

It happened so fast. And we were half a mile down the road before it registered.

Bill slammed the car to a halt. "My God! That was a wolf."

I looked at him. "I saw it, too. Let's go back."

We weren't scared—we were thrilled, fascinated, excited. Wolves were supposed to be long gone in Oregon, yet stories continually surfaced from hunters, backpackers, and fisherman who'd seen them. The naysayers dismissed every alleged wolf sighting as a coyote, or the result of too much peppermint schnapps passed around the campfire.

Bill turned the car around and we headed back up the road.

"Maybe it was a coyote?" I said.

Bill shook his head. "We've both seen hundreds of coyotes. That was a wolf." He looked sideways at me. "Come on, you know how different wolves and coyotes look."

I did. Coyotes are medium-sized and rangy-looking, like scrappy dogs for the most part. Wolves are much bigger, with broad, heavy heads, triangular ruffs, and a bushy tail that's carried high. Coyotes' tails are carried closer to the ground, slumped. A full-grown wolf might top 120 pounds, while an adult coyote is lucky to manage a scruffy forty. As for facial appearance, the difference between a coyote and a wolf is as obvious as that between a bobcat and a cougar.

We backtracked, approaching the turn where we'd seen the wolf. Even if it had been real, I doubted the wolf would still be there. Our car would certainly have scared him back into the trees. And sure enough, the roadside was empty. Bill pulled over. Maybe we'd imagined it. We sighed, disappointed.

Then Bill froze, whispering.

"Look."

I followed his eyes.

The wolf faced us from the other side of the two-lane road, having crossed after we'd driven by. There was no mistaking the full-grown timber wolf. He was a huge animal, standing waist-high and with ruffed chest, broad head, and pads bigger than Bill's hands. His shaggy coat shone in the moonlight, his breath puffing white clouds against the freezing air as we watched each other. I swear, that wolf looked right into our eyes. It was both exquisite and unsettling to be appraised by a wild carnivore. The wolf stood silent and calm, seeming to take our measure. It felt as if we'd been stopped in time, held in our tracks for some otherworldly purpose. A communion of some type was taking place. Surrounded by moonlight and glittering snow, it felt as if we were between worlds, in liminal space.

Then the wolf turned, stealing into the sub-canopy of salal and alder. The night-dark forest swallowed his silver form, and as quickly as the whole episode had begun, it was over.

We sat for a moment, not talking.

Then Bill said, "I knew it! I knew there were wolves in Oregon. Once or twice when I was hunting I've heard them, howling. I knew it!"

"But what's it supposed to mean?" I asked. "What just happened? Didn't you feel it?

"We've seen something most people will never see," said Bill.

Back on the road, we didn't talk much. We were both caught in the experience, in the vision of a gleaming, silver wolf, a wolf that was there when the experts said he shouldn't be, a wolf that stood and looked into our eyes, just as we looked into his. It was as pure a moment as any I've ever experienced.

. . . .

Wolves tend to inspire a wide range of human emotion, most notably fear. Humans and wolves often share territory, and while the wolf doesn't worry too much about us, we fear the massive canine, known for carrying off farm animals, terrorizing the countryside, and even giving rise to the legends of were-creatures, werewolves being the best-known.

Wolves feature large in many magickal and cultural legends. The twins Romulus and Remus, sons of Mars and a Vestal Virgin, were raised by wolves and went on to found Rome; the feast of Lupercalia includes symbolic reference to the twins and their wolven family. In Norse myth, Fenris the wolf is created by Loki as a trickster, while Odin's two wolves—Skoll and Hati (repulsion and hatred)—spend their time trying to bite chunks out of the sun and noon, hoping to return the world to darkness. The Christian tradition paints the wolf as dangerous and adversarial; but many Native American tribes see the wolf as an intelligent teacher, full of wisdom, cunning, and compassion.

A totem animal is one with which you feel a strong connection of kinship and identity.

Today, we know wolves to be extremely intelligent and consider them civilized for the societal and multileveled behavioral hierarchy they build within their packs. Choosing a leader—the alpha—and assigning roles to each pack member, wolves function cooperatively, living and hunting together as a community and showing an amazing gamut of emotion.

Wolf Magick

For magickal folk, wolves can be both totem and spirit animals. A totem animal is one with which you feel a strong connection of kinship and identity. Most people actively seek totem animals, finding them during a course of intense study, on vision quest, etc. Totems are teachers: through their example, they inspire us to develop certain qualities and recognize specific gifts within ourselves.

While people seek out totems, a spirit animal cannot be sought, but appears when the time is right. A spirit animal may be one that you have not considered before but which presents itself at a time when you are in need of guidance or prepared to take a spiritual or intellectual leap. If totems are teachers, spirit animals are guardians, infusing your soul with gifts and very much becoming a part of you. Spirit animals may accompany you into the spirit realm, and may help you find answers to magickal problems.

Interestingly, I had already adopted the wolf as a totem before the night I saw the wolf on Mt. Hood. But on that night, when the shining lupine appeared in my path and stared into my eyes, I knew that I had also been called by its spirit presence. Soon after, I carried out a ritual in which I acknowledged the wolf's real and spirit presences in my magickal life. Since then, I acknowledge the wolf as my totem—in addition to my two other totems, bear and crow—and as my only spirit guardian. May his path be swift as he runs through snowy forests, leaving a trail of silvery shadows in the night!

Susan "Moonwriter" Pesznecker's *complete bio appears on page 81.*

Illustration: Tina Fong

Green Witchcraft

Ellen Dugan

Green magick is not so much a "tradition" as it is a magickal and a spiritual way of life. A green witch may be a garden witch, a cottage witch, a kitchen witch, Celtic witch, a self-taught eclectic, or even a traditional witch (a person that has taken formal training into a specific tradition, such as Gardnerian, Alexandrian, Feri, Dianic, or Cabot). The mantle of green magick slips easily over all these practices.

Green practitioners are clever and adaptable. They may live in the city or tucked into the suburbs. Their physical location does not define them. These green folks, from every profession, location, or climate, choose to work with magickal energies and nature as they find them. Green practitioners connect with their living and working environment because of their ethics, and because they have an affinity to the powers of the natural world. Their physical climate and personal relationship with the energy that is available within their surroundings are taken into consideration. Green magick is an intensely personal path.

Natural Magick

Practitioners of witchcraft use the natural energies within the elements of Earth, Air, Fire, and Water and combine them with their personal power to create positive change and to accomplish a magickal goal. In green magick, the witch becomes the link between the energies and magick of the natural world and the mundane world. The witch

> **To effectively use green magick, you ... have to feel it in your heart.**

becomes a sort of bridge between these two worlds and they carry information back and forth. This connection allows love and knowledge to flow back and forth between the magickal and the mundane worlds, bringing hope, peace, healing, and positive energy to each.

According to folklore, witches were referred to as "hedge jumpers." It's a term that points to witches' knowledge of the green world and their ability to jump the hedge or boundaries between the two worlds. Hedge witches were thought to be able to travel back and forth between the physical world and the spirit world at will. They were not leaping back and forth between the different planes; however, they practiced their craft with one foot firmly planted in each world, thereby creating that spiritual bridge. This description is still used to illustrate the path of the witch.

The Green Magick Path

The green path of magick has its roots in time-honored Craft practices, yet there is plenty of room for personalization and adaptation to the environment where the witch lives. This path closely follows the cycles of nature, life, the wheel of the year, herbalism, the groves, and the garden. Wherever you live, you would incorporate the climate variations, flora and fauna, and the seasons you are familiar with into your magickal practices. To be a green witch simply means going with what you've got, adapting to your surroundings, improvising when necessary, and studying your environment so you know which earthy, natural supplies are available.

To effectively use green magick, you must know that it springs from two sources: the heart and the mind. You have to feel it in your heart. You have to know that if you believe that change is possible, then, so shall it be. A witch who uses green magick will work to create and to preserve balance within, to find harmony with their own mundane and magickal communities, and to celebrate their connection with the natural world. Sounds like a tall order, doesn't it? Never fear, it can be done, and it can be done beautifully.

No matter where you live, what your experience level, or what variety of magickal tradition you observe, you will find something on the green path that will complement your own magickal practice. This will enable you to create a deeper connection to your earth-based religion.

Traveling On the Green Magick Path

It takes a brave soul to travel the green and natural path of the witch. To study and practice a religion that is often misunderstood or scoffed at takes courage. Your daring and determination will serve you well as you practice green magick. Take the opportunity for some quality one-on-one time with the natural world. Plant a garden or a container of herbs and see what lessons they have to teach you. Talk to the trees and get to know the flora and fauna of your neighborhood. This will give you the opportunity to discover your own unique connection to nature, and to become familiar with some of the herbs and botanicals in the plant kingdom.

Your success will depend on your willingness to get in there and experiment. Plan on tracking your spells and carefully watch and record the outcome of your green magick with plants. Remember that plants are intricately intertwined into all magicks and earth religions. They offer supplies, inspiration, and lessons for those folks who know how to open their hearts and listen.

There are great rewards and impressive magickal results for those individuals who possess the inclination for green magick. So, dare to explore the enchanted groves and dig deeper into the magickal gardens of the green world and discover the wonder and magick that the natural world can offer you as a green witch.

By exploring the green path of magick, and by listening to your own heart, you will gain a deep and meaningful sense of connection to nature and to the spirit world. This sense of reverence is but a tool and another magickal lesson to be learned. When you acknowledge and work with green magickal forces and the energies of nature, you are on a less traveled route. Those who honor the powers of nature, green magick, and the old ways of the wise woman and the cunning man gain a connection to the magickal world that is amazing and personal. Whether you are part of a large pagan community or on your own, whether you work in a traditional coven or an open eclectic circle, a green witch is truly never alone.

So be at home and know that you are most welcome in the natural world of the witch. For when you enter the wild places and look for green magick, you'll be working hand in hand with nature. Know that the spirits of the wise ones will join you in the gardens, groves, hedgerows, forests, and woodlands. Hail, and welcome.

Ellen Dugan, *also known as the Garden Witch, lives in Missouri with her husband and three children. A practicing witch for over twenty-four years and a psychic-clairvoyant, Ellen received her master gardener status through the University of Missouri and her local county extension office. She teaches classes on witchcraft, magickal herbalism, and practical magick. Look for other articles by Ellen in Llewellyn's annual* Magical Almanac *and* Herbal Almanac. *Visit her Web site at www.geocities. com/edugan_gardenwitch.*

Illustration: Lydia Hess

The Life Cycle of Magickal Groups

Lisa McSherry

When people form a magickal group, the normal processes of group dynamics apply. The group will go through an evolutionary process, likely moving back and forth between several stages (rather than progressing through them) from the time of its formation.

Although these dynamics are easy to see in a group undergoing stress, they are actually happening all the time. All groups, not just those coming together for a magickal purpose, move from being warm and fuzzy, where everyone is their best selves, through chaos and confrontation, and then into a place of true community. This article offers a brief look at each stage as well as suggestions for making each stage progress as smoothly as possible.

Gathering Phase

While traditional psychology and sociology calls the initial stage of a group "forming," I prefer to use the term "gathering." At this earliest stage, members will tend to rely on safe, patterned behavior and look to the group leader for guidance and direction. For many of us, following a leader is an ingrained behavior. Scott Peck calls this stage *pseudocommunity* and says:

> ... members attempt to be an instant community by being extremely pleasant to one another and avoiding all disagreement ... The essential dynamic of pseudocommunity is conflict avoidance. The basic pretense is the denial of individual differences.

This is the time when members are on their best behavior. The environment feels warm and fuzzy, usually because members are doing their best to be liked and to get comfortable with the group as a whole.

The element for this stage is Air. The group is inspired and energized, eager to try new things and move in new directions. Members say things like "I've come home," and "We are all so alike." Everything feels fresh and new; there is a feeling of great freedom and a belief among members that they can be whomever they want in this new community. It is a time associated with dawn, when the sun's first rays appear over the curve of the world.

The main task for the leader(s) or elders of this group is to remember how good this stage of the cycle feels, and that it will not last. Group members desire a safe group. They want to (at least initially) keep things simple and free of controversy.

A Steady Breeze Promotes Comfort

The leader or elders can help the group stay on track by keeping topics focused on why the group is gathering together and learning about one another. This is the time to transmit all the information about "how things are done." Members who are quiet or shy can be encouraged to participate more while the more boisterous members need to learn how to share the stage. A key concept is that the tone and attitude the leader/elders project will guide future behaviors and patterns of response.

Group members often come with unvoiced concerns about acceptance or rejection. They wonder whether joining this group is a risky undertaking. Differences will be smoothed over (or ignored) in the interests of getting along. Some members question whether they are seen as important and whether they can achieve their goals within the group. Still others are afraid to look stupid or feel reluctant to reveal too much (they are here for a purpose, not to make friends, darn it!). Depending on the group's stated purpose, some members wonder if they can achieve what is asked of them. Some of the general characteristics of this stage are listed here.

- Periods of silence and awkwardness

- Impatience on some members' part to "get the ball rolling"

- Confusion about roles

- "Cocktail conversations"—safe levels of conversation

Throughout this stage, rituals to open the group to the inspiration of Mercury or Arianrhod will be especially helpful for managing the group's expectations. Both of these deities are affiliated with inspiration, the element of Air, and communication. They can bring

wisdom to the leader, and assist in the flow of information between group members.

ICEBREAKERS: "GET-TO-KNOW-YOU" GAMES

There are several "get-to-know-you" games that can open your group up with laughter.

Guessing Game

Give everyone a list of questions to ask each other. These might be questions about their Craft name, pets, hobbies, astrology sign, or favorite foods. Pair everyone into two groups: Ss and Qs. The S person remains completely silent while Q asks the questions from the list, and then predicts what the answers will be, writing the predictions down. After a set time limit, have them switch roles. Gather everyone together again and have the pairs introduce one another with their predictions, corrected by their partner.

Sharing Game

Ask everyone, "What made you smile today?" and encourage everyone to share at least one thing.

Pair everyone up and have the pairs stay together until both people find three less obvious things they have in common. (For example, hair color doesn't count, but both discovering that their mother attended Woodstock would count.) When they've found the hidden similarities, have them switch to a new partner. Continue until everyone has made a connection with at least three others. (This exercise is especially fun in a larger gathering.)

Clearing Phase

After the bright promise of the morning, the group must move on to the next stage: clearing. As hard as it is, this stage has to happen. Eventually, those best behaviors wear off and conflicts arise when members admit they have differences. Those differences become more obvious, and sometimes those differences become more important than anything else. After the false similarities of the gathering phase, members frequently feel betrayed when another person seems to change his or her mind. This feeling is more prominent for members who have self-esteem issues or difficult family lives. Suddenly, wide swings in behavior occur, with some members acting mute while others attempt to dominate all conversations. Either silence or dominance is a reaction to feeling discomfort about having to "deal" with conflict to any degree.

Personal will begins to manifest itself at this stage, and members begin to stand up for themselves—not always at the best time, however. This stage corresponds with the element of Fire. Things start getting a little hot in the group as the need to be "right" and convince others that they are wrong is asserted.

For the leader(s) or elders of this group, the task is to let events unfold, as difficult as that is when their authority is challenged. A reminder to the group of the rules of tolerance and respect may minimize chaos or harm to other members. Some leaders feel the need to create more and more rules in order to impose structure on something that is, essentially, uncontrollable. It is best to resist the urge to apply controls. Instead, try to recognize differences as distinct without attaching either good or bad as a judgment. Show respect for everyone, and model tolerance (for example, by remembering that one person's norm may not be the same as another's).

Group members do best in this difficult environment when they start to mold their feelings, ideas, attitudes, and beliefs to suit the group's organization. This is not an act of giving up the self so much as it is an alignment with shared goals. Members must move from a testing and proving mentality to one focused on problem solving. At this stage, simply listening is the best way to help the group move on to the next stage.

ACTIVE LISTENING

This exercise assists in the clearing stage as it allows people to feel a connection to one another that can transcend the fire. Arbitrarily sitting down for a conversation like this will feel awkward at first, but practice will bring comfort.

Divide the group into subgroups of three, each of whom will choose the role of Speaker, Listener, or Observer. (Depending on the number of participants, the leader might join one of the subgroups, or just wander around listening in.) The Speaker talks about something important for no more than five minutes: job, family, a decision, a question, etc. (The exercise is better if the topic is something the Speaker really cares about.) The Listener does their best to listening actively, using eye contact, body language, silences, and verbal encouragers. The Observer pays attention to the Listener's verbal and nonverbal skills, counting as many of those behaviors—eye contact, body posture, verbal encouragers, topic jumps—as they can manage (and still be relatively accurate).

When the Speaker is finished, the Listener discusses the experience with the two other members of the subgroup by asking "What was comfortable? Difficult?" and "Did you stay with the Speaker?" Then the Speaker will share his or her feelings about the Listener's listening—whether or not they felt listened to, or found the exercise helpful. The Observer will then share observations. This sharing process should take about five minutes.

Everyone changes places. Have the Listener become the Speaker, the Speaker the Observer, and the Observer the Listener. Go through the five minutes of talking and listening and five minutes of exchanging remarks twice more so that each person takes each role once. The entire practice session should take about twenty-five minutes.

When everyone has taken a turn at the three roles, reform into the larger group and share your experiences. How are these skills relevant to your work? Where else would they be useful? Go around the group so that participants have a chance to share at least one thing they have learned about themselves in this exercise.

Working with the Fire gods and goddesses can assist the group throughout this stage, especially when wisdom to understand the deeper needs of the group is needed. In particular, Pele, who dances the destructive lava up from the earth's core and in doing so creates new islands. Any deity who deals with creating paths (Horus comes to mind) is good to work with for guidance through the clearing phase.

The Building Phase

After the chaos and unhappiness of the clearing phase, moving on to the building phase comes as a relief. Here we begin the process of growth and in some ways this can be the most challenging part of the cycle.

Ideally, group members are now actively acknowledging all contributions and there is an active sense of community building, as well as ongoing problem solving. By now, the group has learned that disagreement does not mean rejection, and deep feelings of trust can begin to form. It is at this stage (assuming the group gets this far) that members begin to experience a sense of true community (as opposed to the pseudocommunity of gathering).

The element of Water is associated with building. This is the time when we begin to deal with the truth that lies beneath our surface selves. Here, unconscious patterns of behavior and needs are more obvious, and real sharing of emotions and intimacy takes place. Much as water pours from a jar, preconceptions and prior negative training are washed away. Group members finally experience one another emotionally, rather than sharing only those parts of themselves that are deemed acceptable.

For the leader(s) or group elders, guiding the group through this stage has new challenges. Although individual group members may see glimpses of the group's potential for true community, it is not yet fully real. Many negative patterns and past-based behaviors are still around. These habits of thought and feeling persist in hindering members' ability to experience the full potential of working within a healthy group. Here, it is the leader's task to understand that sometimes it is necessary to take a step back and clarify needs and expectations before the group can continue forward again. (Not only is it necessary, it is healthy.) The leader should be constantly asking

- are individuals empowered?

- are individuals more important than the group? (The goal is to find a balance of tension between individual and group needs.)

- are tension and conflict viewed as natural elements in the problem-solving process?

- are openness, directness, probing, and emotions not only acceptable, but necessary?

- what is the level of secrecy within the group?

- is independent critical thinking supported?

- is there unconditional respect and personal regard for each member?

- is the process more important than the results?

- does there always have to be a solution?

- do members maintain a healthy balance between life in and life outside the group?

For leaders, it is vitally important to remember that this stage is difficult to maintain. The established group members will frequently "backslide" into the chaos of the clearing phase and new members can easily precipitate a return to the gathering phase.

Group members may experience persistent fear about expressing true feelings that may result in disaster, either because the truth would provoke argument within the group (and a slide back into clearing), or because the response isn't what they wanted. The primary task for members is to do their own work and find their own authenticity and truth. In doing so, they will come to understand others, and the results are a safe space and comfort. Almost inevitably, in this stage, trust issues arise. Treating members with compassion allows for deeper levels of trust to evolve. Here, members learn to change preconceived ideas or opinions and actively ask questions of one another. A sign that the group is healthy is when members seek to share leadership—not for power, but for shared responsibility.

Trust Building Exercises

These exercises encourage group members to build trust in one another and thereby deepen their connections to each other.

Taffy Pull

First, ask everyone to remove sharp jewelry and other adornments. Divide the group into two teams: Taffy and Pullers. The Taffy people sit down and link arms, legs, and bodies into a tangled mess. The Pullers try to gently pull the Taffy people apart into human-sized bits. Remind the Pullers that the best taffy is made by using smooth stretches; if you pull too hard the taffy will snap. Members of the Taffy group can decide how much they want to remain a part of the taffy mass.

Trust Circle

Everyone stands in a tight circle, shoulder to shoulder, facing in. Have one person stand in the center of the circle, with his feet together and arms next to his sides. When he is ready, have him close his eyes and gently fall to one side of the circle. Group members gently catch the man and pass him from person to person, across and around the circle (The person shouldn't have to move his feet much, or at all.) Keep the circle small. The goal is to gently pass, not throw, the person back and forth. Be gentle. If some members are unable to "let go," other group members can honor their strength and ability to care for themselves by stating their needs.

Trust Walk

Have the group line up and hold hands. Designate one person at the end of the line as the leader. Have everyone close their eyes (or be blindfolded) except the leader, who will lead the group over, under, around, and through various obstacles. The leader guides the person directly behind them, using vocal and/or tactile directions. That person must do the same to the "blind" person behind them, and on down the line. This exercise can also be done in pairs.

Water deities are wonderful guides throughout this stage. The mythological cycle of Isis and Osiris offers useful insights about moving forward, then back, and then forward again through periods of transformation.

The Community Phase

Every group will go through the first three stages—gathering, clearing, and building—repeatedly. In many groups, a large number of the members will go from gathering into clearing and then back to gathering several times over before finally moving on to the building phase. It is also commonplace for groups to move from building back to clearing on regular occasions—particularly if it is a task-oriented magickal group. After a task is accomplished, the group drops back into clearing or gathering until it redefines its new goal.

The next phase—*community*—is rarely attained.

With community, we see individual members who are self-assured and confident; the need for group approval was left in the past. Members are highly task- and people-oriented, and they have a strong sense of unity. The group identity is clear, morale is high, and loyalty is intense. Differences of any sort are accepted and valued, rather than hidden or highlighted. They know that they have explored together, fought with one another, earned respect, and made a place with one another. The group has found its center. As befits that sense of stability, this stage corresponds with the element of Earth.

Leader(s) or elders of a group in the community phase have a strong feeling of accomplishment. Now, the biggest pitfall is that the group may feel complaisant and start to believe they are at the end of a cycle; that the journey is completed and there are no further destinations. Not true! The community phase is not a goal, like winning a race, or completing a project; it is a way station along the journey. It is likely that the group will shift into other stages as group members come and go, or the group's focus and intent deviates from the original. The leader may plan for a recycling to reenergize and reconnect with the energy of gathering, for example.

Group members may begin to ask themselves, "What part of me must die so that my true self can be born?" This is frequently when they will answer by making large changes within their lives. A woman in an emotionally dead long-term relationship seeks out counseling. A man who allowed his wife to gain full custody of their children may explore the possibility of sharing responsibility with

her once again. Someone who never saw herself as a writer may begin to write a book. These changes are, as you may expect, painful for the individual and often disruptive for the group. The process of maintaining the balance between individual and group needs will require attention and care on the part of all members. Here, in fact, is where the line between leader and member can be very thin, or even nonexistent.

Deities most closely identified with the element of Earth offer guidance through this stage. I recommend Demeter and Cernunnos, in particular. Expanding your circle to include the surrounding community and thinking of continuity are topics all members are encouraged to consider throughout this stage.

The Releasing Phase

The final stage of the cycle, in more ways than one, is *release*. Technically, all groups go through this stage, but many do not do so formally or with intent. I believe that release requires the formal closing of the group and the ending of current relationships.

This is one of the most difficult phases of the life cycle of a group; it's where the pain may be greatest for all members. Many groups will end (generally while moving through clearing or building), but a planned end calls for a different mind-set and focus. Release, at its best, requires a deep honesty and consensus. Ending a group out of pique, or politics, is not release.

The most effective interventions in this stage are those that facilitate task termination and the disengagement process. All members engage in this process, opening deeply and connecting as closely as they can in preparation for their disengagement.

Spirit is the guiding element for this stage, the energy that assists us as we move from the physical plane to that of the immaterial. Our bonds, once so strong and supportive, become memories and lessons learned. A planned end usually includes recognition for participation and achievement and an opportunity for members to say personal goodbyes. Concluding a group can create some apprehension—in effect, a minor crisis. The termination of the group is a regressive movement from giving up control to giving up inclusion in the group.

There is no single deity to ask for guidance throughout this period, so prayers to the One, the All, or the Source may be especially useful.

Conclusion

One point to not lose in all of this is that a magickal group's life cycle is not a wheel to be moved through, or a circle to watch. Rather, it is a progression of phases that overlap and that are ever-changing.

May your cycle be informative!

Lisa McSherry, *a practicing witch for more than twenty-five years, is the author of* Magickal Connections: Creating a Healthy and Lasting Spiritual Group (*New Page,* 2007) *and* The Virtual Pagan: Exploring Wicca, and Paganism Through the Internet (*Weiser,* 2002). *The senior editor and owner of* Facing North: A Community Resource (*www. facingnorth.net*), *she is a frequent contributor to other Pagan publications and can be reached at lisa@cybercoven.org.*

Illustrations: Tim Foley

Magical Feet

Spiffy Galoot

Feeling blah? Dreary? I found a magical cure: a *pedi*-cure. P*ed* is short for "pedestrian," which in turn is synonymous with "blah." The antonym for blah is "electrifying!" A *ped-i-cure*, therefore, is literally a cure for the blahs, an electrifying ritual. Follow-up by shopping for the perfect high heels and bring the ceremony gleefully full-circle.

In Asian cultures, foot scrubbing—cleansing and soothing—is an end-of-the-day ritual that's comparable to our evening bubble bath. W*ai*, a Thai foot massage ritual, includes formal tea service. The Thai foot massage originated in China, and it has been practiced at least five thousand years. My pedicurist, Kanya, is from Thailand, where foot massage is offered on nearly every city block. Kanya stretches my muscles to open Sen energy lines. With a stick, she beats foot reflex points that enliven my internal organs.

Foot washing is a tradition that is observed globally. A random collection of such rituals follows.

Foot-Washing Rituals

A SCOTTISH BRIDE'S RITUAL

This foot-washing ritual is a tradition for brides in the Orkney Islands, off Scotland's shores. The bridesmaids warm a tub of wine. The father of the bride takes off the bride's shoes. Then, her mother pulls the stockings off and rotates the bride's feet over the wine tub clockwise. Mom calls for a blessing while patting each foot, then slips both into the wine, surreptitiously dropping in a ring as well. The maids-in-waiting scrub the bride's feet while fishing for the ring, and whoever discovers it will be the next to marry.

If you plan to marry soon, consider incorporating "fit-washin" night into your ceremonies. Don't forget to have Dad hoist the wine cask out into the sunshine and leave it there for twelve hours; and all the while, guarding it against the gaze of dogs.

RELIGIOUS RITUAL

Christian mythology includes two examples of prayerful foot washing, normally the task of a personal slave. Mary Magdalene used costly perfume to wash the feet of Jesus, then dried them with her hair. Then, on the night before his death, Jesus, in turn, washed the feet of his disciples. Jesus performed his foot-washing during a dinner open only to his disciples, ostensibly twelve men. The tradition that he washed no women's feet (genitals, remember?) led to the Vatican's pronunciation that Roman Catholic Holy Thursday foot washing prohibited washing any women's (sexy) feet—filthy man feet only, please. Some dioceses sorta, kinda forget about this rule, and the priest humbly cleanses every foot presented.

The Islamic *wadu* requires every Muslim to wash his or her own feet five times a day. To accomodate ubiquitous Muslim taxi-drivers, the Kansas City International Airport added foot-washing basins to restrooms because common restroom sinks were hardly conducive to foot bathing.

Foot-washing Services

Homeless folks often wander barefoot, or in holey shoes that contribute to soiled feet. UC Berkeley funds a clinic where undergrads use rubber-ducky-handled scrub brushes and pink bars of soap to cleanse the feet of the Bay area's displaced people. For the recipients, many of whom arrive daily for this care, it provides a rare chance for human touch. For the volunteers, the charity enlarges their spirits, requites bad karma, and magically bonds them to otherwise outcast citizens.

Honoring Mothers

A Chinese Mother's Day festival in Chunan Township includes an "Honor Parents by Foot-Washing" ceremony, during which participants wash their mothers' feet and rub them dry. This turnabout harkens back to the parental care these mothers gave their kids when they ran inside dirty-footed from a day of barefoot play.

The Right Foot

Horse-drawn carriages of upperclass Europeans carried a footman whose duty it was to ensure that no one entered a room with the left foot first. It was believed that bad luck would befall the house where someone "started on the wrong foot."

Pythagorus taught that "One must put the right shoe on first," but he required his followers to wash the left foot first. (Next time you have a pedicure, notice which foot your caregiver begins with. Ask her or him why that foot was chosen: you may be privy to some ancient ritual, novel to you.)

Buddha's image was taboo in the early years, so artists symbolized Gautama by carving just his footprints engraved with the Buddhist wheel and other symbols.

You might wonder why the left foot was dangerous. Well, the word *left* derives from the Latin word for *sinister*. The *right*-eous in Greek Christianity sit at the right hand and foot of Yahweh, while the evil sit in judgment on his left.

Foot-tickled Trivia

Footprints retain the essence of their maker, much like a hair represents the whole person in ritual. When you intentionally muss up a footprint, you injure its owner.

Fossilized footprints are revered by scientists and mystics alike. The 3.2 million-year-old footprints of our ancestress Lucy were discovered in Ethiopia. Newer footprints, dated at 38,500 years old, were found in 2003. Three sets of human footprints, which natives refer to as "devils trails," are immortalized in ash on the side of a volcano in southern Italy.

According to Judaic folklore, Adam, the first man, left a large footprint on Adam's Peak, a Sri Lankan mountain. Buddhists disagree, insisting it's a footprint of the sage himself. Hindus know that Shiva left the print there. Sri Lankan Sloth Bears neither argue about this nor care.

Not to be out-immortalized, Satan left another footprint in the paving of a church in Munich. The impression is called *Teufelstritt*— the Devil's Footstep.

Even Jesus, risen bodily into heaven, left a couple of footprints behind. You can step into them at the Church of Domine Quo Vadis near Rome.

Whose footprints are housed in the Ka'ba, Islam's most sacred structure? Not Mohammed's. Abraham's footprints impressed in stone are safeguarded in a domed sanctuary called the Station of Abraham, and are among Muslims' holiest relics. Mohammed's footprints are enshrined on Jerusalem's Dome of the Rock, at the site where Abraham prepared to sacrifice Isaac. Mohammed made the indentation when he rose to heaven from the Rock.

Buddha was so enlightened that he didn't even leave footprints. Instead, golden lotuses sprang up each time Buddha's foot touched the ground. Buddha's image was taboo in the early years, so artists symbolized Gautama by carving just his footprints engraved with the Buddhist wheel and other symbols. Again, the part stood for the whole. Buddha's pseudo-footprints are revered throughout Asia.

Celebrity saints, like Johnny Depp and Paris Hilton, have pressed their miraculous footprints in the concrete outside Grauman's Chinese Theater. But the most precious relics are created by grandchildren smudging their inky toes and heels onto their birth certificates or into safe-and-sane plaster. Yogic gazing at these tiny prints induces states of rapture not achievable even by platform Gucci kneeboots, or prayer and meditation.

Way Too Sexy for Your Feet

Want to cool down the hot pants of lovers traveling without you? Surreptitiously have them step foot into earth, then collect the soil. Like a Zuni Indian, you'll innoculate them against seduction on their trip.

Suppose your lover's foolin' around with another. You'd like to banish the cad and see him or her wander solo from now on, never again finding love. Hoodoo *foot track magic* can accomplish this. While the offender is in your home, walk backwards from your doorstep, sprinkling *hot foot powder*—available online. Once the two-timer exits and his or her footsteps cross the powder path, your ex will never be able to return to you, and will wander alone hereafter.

Mississppi Blues artist Robert Johnson mourned his honey's use of hot foot powder in "Hellbound on My Trail" (1936):

> *You sprinkled hot foot powder all around your daddy's door.*
> *It keep me with ramblin' mind, every old place I go.*

Annoying visitors and door-to-door sales reps may also be repelled with some foot track magic. You can probably imagine other uses.

Feet of the Gods and Goddesses

Goddess and godlike feet play central roles in global mythologies. Hindu's supreme God, Vishnu, sleeps upon the endless serpent, while the goddess Lakshmi, massages his feet.

The Celtic god-king Math could survive only so long as he kept his feet in the lap of a virgin, removing them only for military campaigns.

The Norse god Vidar revenges his father Odin's death by pressing his foot down upon the jaw of Fenrir, the chaos wolf, killing him.

Jason, the Greek Argonaut, was able to overthrow King Pelias only because he was wearing one sandal, as the seers had prophesied. He'd lost his other sandal while gallantly ferrying an aged woman across a river. The woman was a goddess in disguise.

Examine the feet of your goddess statues. Are the icons barefoot? Greek marbles portray unshod goddesses. Why? Surely, the feminine foot is in itself a work of art, but there's another reason. The tradition stems from sumptuary laws regulating personal expenditure on clothing. Greek women were only allowed to wear three garments at a time, so most women walked barefoot. Their goddesses could do no less.

What Bare Feet Reveal about Us

If you're lucky enough to have an extra toe or two, you'll be lucky all your life; and if you were born breech, you're a "footer," and will be a powerful healer.

Barefoot marching was used to punish the marines of Rome's Emperor Claudius I. When his marines dared request reimbursement for worn-out boots, Claudius broke their quasi-union by confiscating their footwear.

Baring one's feet before entering holy places is a global tradition held for millenia. Pythagorus taught his adherents to enter temples barefoot. The reverent remove their footwear and leave it outside before entering Buddhist, Hindu, and Muslim edifices. Many householders request visitors to remove their shoes when entering their homes, for purposes of cleanliness and godliness.

A barefoot bride may be opening the door to a stormy, unblessed marriage. Get those glass slippers out.

Shoe Magic

Study a pair of your old leather shoes. You may see permanent scruff marks, a stretch over a big toe, a heel worn down more on one side than the other. This shabby chic might explain why folks have long believed old shoes retain not just the idiosyncratic shape of their occupying feet, but the essence of their owners' souls. By inheriting your mother's shoes, besides following in her footsteps, you are heir to her accumulated luck.

To ensure your dearly departed safely crosses over to the other side, bury or cremate the beloved wearing shoes.

Bad Luck Shoes

If you've had a run of bad luck lately and aren't planning to wear some footwear soon, take the pair up to the roof of your condo and leave it awhile to fend off evil spirits. But come Friday the Thirteenth, go back up and get those shoes; wear them that day to ward off an accident.

Never put your shoes on a table unless you're itching for a fight: they'll attract a domestic quarrel and a thunderstorm to boot.

Don't run to answer the phone with only one shoe on: one year of bad luck will run after you.

Good Luck Shoes

Worried about goblins invading your home at Winter Solstice? You may have seen the movie. Imitate the ancient Greeks: burn a pair of old shoes in your fireplace, pit, or cauldron. Goblins will disperse.

Tuck some maidenhair fern in your slippers and you'll soon discover treasure. Sprinkle salt and pepper in your left shoe to attract money.

Healthy Shoes

When your stomach aches, drink oregano tea, then place a heavy boot on your tummy. The boot will sop up your discomfort, and the oregano will do its magic in your digestive tract.

Prohibited Shoes

Fourteenth-century gigolos wore "polaines," shoes with twenty-four-inch toe extensions. Imagine to what uses these may have been put. Clergy members forbid this phallic footware, fearing it induced pagan penis worship. Priests went so far as to blame polaines for the Black Plague.

In fifteenth-century Siena, prostitutes alone could don slippers in public. Chaste women who emulated their passionate sisters were excommunicated from the Catholic Church. Worse, they brought the law down upon their husbands and fathers who were supposed

to be controlling their women. The men were punished by loss of property and title, and if they had neither of these, they were simply put to death. (And you thought *you* were *dying for* those Marc Jacob black-and-white pony slippers.)

In 1530, the Bishop of Lincoln, England, wrote to the abbess of Vinestoww Convent and ordered the nuns not to wear crested or slashed shoes. As no one was allowed to enter cloisters, it isn't known whether they complied.

Put on your cross-trainers and you're following the advice of a Venetian ambassador of 1618: he suggested all gentle women wear men's shoes.

Noble Venetian women of the seventeenth century never appeared in public except on tall "chopines," with soles almost as high has their feet were long, and upon which they couldn't walk unless supported on both sides. Pull out your own platforms from the 1970s, and you'll honor your high-steppin' ancestresses. Why did Florence eventually outlaw the towering chopines? Too many ladies fell over.

Mesmerizing high-heeled shoes were banned in seventeenth-century New Jersey. A law was passed in 1670 that stated:

> Be it resolved that all women, of whatever age, rank, profession; whether virgin maids or widows; that shall betray into matrimony any of His Majesty's male subjects, by scents . . . artificial teeth . . . or high-heeled shoes, shall incur the penalty of the laws now in force against witchcraft and sorcery, and the marriage shall stand null and void.

If that law still stands, it may be an easy way out of a bad marriage. Just show photos of your wedding shoes, and voila—nullification!

During World War II, the U.S. government used the excuses of rationing and a national emergency to control the height of high heels. Rather than reduce interest in high heels, this only escalated their popularity. So did the association of high heels with sado-masochistic eroticism.

If all these laws against high heels have convinced you of their sorcerous properties, try wearing twelve-inch spikes for your next amorous encounter and discover what magic may ensue.

We bare our feet to ground ourselves in Mother Earth. We shod them to protect us from the underworld. Our two personal magic carpets take us anywhere we desire to go.

Poetry is measured in feet. Magical rituals with stockings and shoes ensure true love and happy marriage. Embalmers slip sandals on our sleeping loved ones to protect their feet as they traverse the afterlife.

. . . .

I've barely dipped a toe into the ocean of foot symbolism in religion, mythology, and culture. But perhaps that's enough, as a single toe dipped in the river of Mother Ganges cleanses us of every sin.

I hope that as you've eenie-meenie-miney-moed through this little article, some magic ideas have adhered to the soles of your blessed feet.

Spiffy Galoot *is a theomicrist who pokes fun at other people's belief systems in lieu of embarking on her own spiritual quest. Spiffy clings to the brink of the earth in a Californian beach town. (Sometimes, she lets go.) Sightings of Spiffy include Manhattan Island and Monterey Bay. If you're having trouble with your twelve-step program because you don't believe in a higher power, Spiffy can help. She will be your higher power and cradle you in her skeptical heart. Spiffy's Cathedral of Theomicry resides at http:// www.Godishness.com. Hope to see you there.*

Illustrations: Tina Fong

Witchcraft Essentials

PRACTICES, RITUALS & SPELLS

Magical Perceptions

Elizabeth Barrette

Magic is a subtle force with infinite manifestations. It moves through both physical and metaphysical layers of reality. When we encounter magic, it makes itself known to us in many different ways. This causes a lot of confusion, and even underlies some arguments that magic isn't "real." We know that different people perceive the same magic in different ways. Some people find it easy to sense magic, while others find it difficult or impossible. An exploration of the field of magical perceptions will indicate why these things are so.

What Are "Perceptions?"

They are similar to our physical senses, only more subtle; and it is through our subtle senses that we sense magic. Some perceptive senses have become quite famous. The *taisch* (or second sight) of the Celts is one example. Second sight gives glimpses of the future or the present in distant places. These glimpses are often visual or auditory, and they may warn of danger. A sixth sense allows one to detect, and sometimes to communicate with, disembodied entities.

The family of psychic senses, also called "far senses" or "clear senses" includes clairvoyance (clear seeing), clairaudience (clear hearing), clairalience (clear smelling), clairgustance (clear tasting), clairtangency (clear touching), and clairsentience (clear knowing). They are analogous to the physical senses, and allow people to sense ordinary things at a distance, as well as to sense magical things.

Looking at a randomly moving pattern, such as waves or leaves in the wind, also helps create images in your mind.

From these examples, you can tell we lack a vocabulary that applies exclusively to magical senses. Second sight and a sixth sense are just numbered references based on the physical senses. Our analog senses function much like their physical counterparts.

Subtle senses often follow elemental associations. People with a strong air affinity may have clairaudience, while people with strong fire may have clairvoyance, and those with water may have clairgustance, those with earth may have clairtangency, and spirit may have clairsentience. In books, magic is almost always described visually, but not everyone has visual perceptions. I've known aromatherapists who could smell magic, and healers who could feel energy flows with their hands. If you have trouble perceiving magic, try detecting it through other sensory ranges.

VISUAL PERCEPTIONS

Visual perception, or clairvoyance, reveals light and shadows, colors, shapes, and images of magical energies or entities. Second sight usually includes imagery, showing distant people, places, or times. It can include sounds or other input as well. Aura vision reveals the energy fields around other people, powerful objects, or places. Astral vision reveals disembodied or invisible beings, and allows vision while traveling out-of-body. Symbolic vision shows images that reveal hidden information in a nonliteral way; for example, a liar might suddenly appear to have a forked tongue.

Magic can manifest visually in many ways. Colors in an aura or other energy can indicate mood, intensity, or type of magic. For instance, healing magic often appears green. Power can appear as a light or glow. Low power or negative energy may look like a shadow or black patch. A shadow that moves against the light is almost always magical (and can be dangerous). Pools or lines of magic can create shimmers or ripples around them as they distort the light, much like heat waves. Visual perceptions may also create whole images of objects or scenes, or they may reveal things that are otherwise invisible.

Shifting Focus

You can adjust your physical eyes to focus on objects close to you (making distant objects fuzzy) or on objects far away (making nearby ones fuzzy). Both the near and far objects are equally "real," just not all clear at the same time. Similarly, when your physical vision is fuzzy, your mystical vision tends to sharpen. To practice your Sight, let your eyes use soft focus. (If you wear glasses or contact lenses,

simply remove them!) Looking at a randomly moving pattern, such as waves or leaves in the wind, also helps create images in your mind. Look at the soft-edged world to search for signs of magic. Do you see any bright spots or dark shadows without an obvious source, shimmers or heat waves, halos of color, and so forth?

AUDITORY PERCEPTIONS

Clairaudience is the ability to hear sounds from distant times or places. Some other senses frequently manifest in the audio range, too. A warning of danger may come to you as sound, like an alarm bell, siren, or shouted warning. Telepathy and animal communication often sound like voices, which can be internal or external.

Magic can make various sounds, some especially common, of voices that are intelligible only through clairaudience. Bird or animal calls, water running, wind, and other natural sounds may carry mystical messages, or you may hear the sounds themselves, magically, when no mundane source is present. Mundane sounds with specific meanings may be used by your subconscious to represent a message: if you hear a phone ringing when one isn't, someone may be trying to contact you psychically. Magic energy itself may have a sound—a low hum when inactive, engine sounds or drumming when active, a growl or staticky crackle when hostile, a purr or music when beneficent, etc.

Sound Spirals

You need at least ten minutes when you will not be disturbed. Sit or lie down in a comfortable position. Relax. First, listen to the sounds within your own body, ignoring all other sounds. Next, shift your attention just outside your body. Identify the sound nearest to you and listen to it. Then spiral outwards again to the next sound. Keep expanding your range of attention until you reach the farthest limit of your hearing. Then gradually spiral inwards until you are listening only to your body's sounds again. Now imagine opening your spirit ears. Does your body have a message for you? Can you hear grass growing or wind whispering? If there are birds or other animals calling, can you understand them? Are the objects on your altar giving off a low hum, like appliances?

Tactile Perceptions

Clairtangency is the ability to feel objects from a distance. We can feel heat, cold, pressure, pain, tickling, and many other sensations. Sometimes telekinesis comes with this ability to feel what is being moved. Psychometry gives impressions of an object's history, ownership, and other details by handling it. Many senses and talents in the healing category function via touch; a healer may be able to diagnose injury or illness by feeling for damage to a person's energy field.

Magic can feel like all kinds of different things. Most commonly, the energy feels like a hot or warm spot compared to ambient temperature. Magic can also feel like static electricity, either the spark jumping or fuzzy feeling, as when you hold your hand near a television screen. It may feel like a vibration, or a magical item may seem to jump in your hand. Magical fields may push or pull on foreign bodies near them, like currents. Hostile magic often feels painful, itchy, nauseating, or otherwise uncomfortable. These symptoms are a warning to retreat and shield immediately. Magic may "feel" slippery or sticky or velvety, and so on.

Feel the Magic Exercise

For this exercise, gather several objects, both magical and mundane. Spread them on a cloth. Close your eyes and sweep your hand, palm down, just above the objects. Do you feel any warm or cold spots, tingling, pulling or pushing, vibration, etc.? Pick up the objects one at a time. As you hold each one, feel for its mystical qualities. Can you sense what it's used for, its history, its owner, or other things about it? This exercise is especially useful with a friend, so each of you can collect items unfamiliar to the other, and tell whether the impressions are accurate.

Olfactory and Gustatory Perceptions

Olfactory perceptions are analogous to smell; gustatory perceptions are analogous to taste. They are presented together because they're closely related, like the two physical senses that detect and identify chemicals and substances. Clairalience, also called clairolfaction, is the ability to smell things at a distance including things not on the material plane. Clairgustance, or clairsavorance, is the ability to taste things in the same fashion. Olfactory and gustatory perceptions often accompany a gift for working with herbs, oils, incenses, and other materials, when smell or taste is an integral part of their magic. Aromatherapists and herbalists may smell or taste the magical qualities of their ingredients while making a special blend.

Magic doesn't seem to have typical smells or tastes of its own. However, there are notable patterns. Some spirits can be identified when a distinctive smell that accompanied them in life, such as perfume or tobacco smoke, is present. Elemental magic often carries the smell of its element—invoke water, and you may smell rain or the ocean. Some deities and types of magic bring floral fragrances. Taste is a subtle and personal cue of intuition, as hinted at in sayings like "sweet success" and "the experience left a bitter taste in his mouth." Enchanted foods may taste richer than normal, or the power may give them a hot, spicy flavor. In general, positive magic tends to manifest pleasant smells or flavors; negative magic tends to manifest unpleasant ones.

The Nose Knows Exercise

Choose a category of item that has fragrance but whose magical use is generally unfamiliar to you, such as flowers or incense. Find six or more different samples. Sniff each in turn. As you inhale, consider what associations the fragrance brings up. What could its magical powers be: love, prosperity, healing, protection, or something else? What element would you associate it with? Write down your perceptions. Then look in a magical reference to compare your notes with the standard correspondences. (For magical tasting, you can repeat this exercise with foods, spices, etc.)

MENTAL PERCEPTIONS

Mental perceptions do not relate directly to any of the physical senses. They cover a range of information and sensations that simply manifest in the mind, often without an obvious source, and in a manner difficult to describe. Clairsentience, or claircognizance, is the central sense of this type—a true knowing of things, which the receiver has not learned through ordinary means. Telepathy may manifest, not as a voice, but simply as awareness of what someone else is thinking. Empathy is a similar awareness of another's emotions rather than thoughts. Precognition, also called premonition or foresight, is the ability to know what may happen before it does. Postcognition is a similar ability focused on areas of the past for which the person was not present. The sixth sense is a general psychic awareness, which may include aspects of physical senses, but often manifests simply as knowing. Another catchall term is anomalous cognition, which simply denotes awareness without specifying how the information was gained—usually when someone is trying to explain away a magical perception that defies mundane explanation!

Knowing Places

Locations often hold imprints of thoughts or emotions. Casual ones may last only minutes, while stronger ones last for hours or days, and intense ones can last centuries. It is the last category that accounts for some "hauntings." Choose a public place such as a park, wedding chapel, or theater; and to minimize distractions, go there when few other people are around. When you're there, close your eyes and be aware of any thoughts or emotions emanating from the location. Does the place feel happy, sad, tense, boisterous? Write down your perceptions. If anything seems as though it might be a strong and lasting impression, consider asking around to discover whether or not anyone else has noticed the same thing.

Enhancement Tools

Certain items can help you develop your subtle senses. Foods, herbs, incense, essential oils, and stones have special qualities. For example, a stone with a natural hole through it allows you to see fairies and other normally invisible things if you look through the hole. Here are some other ideas.

MAGICAL STONES

Magical stones are usually worn as jewelry or kept on an altar or bed stand. Stones to awaken your subtle senses include: amethyst, aquamarine, emerald, lapis lazuli, moldavite, opal, quartz crystal, and sugilite. Stones to strengthen the subtle senses you already have include: azurite, beryl, bloodstone, citrine, jet, moonstone, opal, pearl, quartz crystal, and sapphire. To communicate with animals, use: animal fossils, bird's eye agate, catseye, hawkeye, leopard jasper, ti-

ger's eye or zebra jasper. To communicate with plants, use: amber, crinoid, jet, leaf fossils, moss agate, or petrified wood. To communicate with spirits, try: angelite, celestite, quartz crystal, or staurolite. For clear visions, use: amber, amethyst, fluorite, moonstone, or obsidian.

OILS, PERFUMES, FOODS, AND SPICES

You may want to try wearing essential oils as perfume, or add them to bath water. Good choices include benison (to awaken mental powers); cinnamon (sharpen psychic awareness); jasmine (increase psychic awareness); juniper (aid telepathy and empathy); lemon (clarify visions); magnolia (expand psychic awareness); peppermint (add strength); sandalwood (expand psychic awareness); and tuberose (soothe restless senses).

Plants can help in many ways, too. To improve psychic powers, eat these foods: celery, grapes, mustard, orange, tangerine, and vanilla. To strengthen psychic powers, burn incense simples and blends, such as: bistort and frankincense, camphor, celery seeds and orris, cinnamon, elecampane, mace, mastic, mugwort and sandalwood, rowan (leaves and berries), star anise, or stillengia. Herbs may be carried or consumed in various forms; here is a list of useful ones.

- Bay leaves in a dreampillow bring prophetic dreams. In tea, they enhance clairvoyance.

- Bladderwrack carried in a sachet can strengthen psychic powers.

- Buchu tea helps foretell the future.

- Catnip enables psychic communication with cats.

- Citron, when eaten, can increase psychic powers.

- Eyebright may be carried in a sachet to increase psychic powers. An infusion, when applied to the eyelids repeatedly for some time, can induce clairvoyance.

- Galangal worn in a sachet aids psychic development.

- Honeysuckle heightens psychic powers. Lightly crush the fresh flowers and rub them on your forehead.

- Horehound candy is a cough drop; it opens subtle senses.

- Iris flowers help while you're practicing your subtle senses.

- Lemongrass tea aids the development of psychic powers.

- Uva ursa in a sachet increases psychic powers.

- Marigold scattered under the bed brings psychic dreams, both precognition and postcognition; it is especially useful for identifying a thief who has robbed you.

- Mugwort stuffed in a dreampillow aids prophetic dreams; burn it during scrying rituals; use it as an infusion to wash scrying mirrors, crystal balls, etc.; and drink it as an infusion before using your subtle senses.

- Peppermint in a dreampillow encourages precognitive dreams.

- Rose can bring prophetic dreams by drinking a tea made from rose hips or rose buds.

- Rowan wood may be carried to increase psychic powers. It's also used for magic wands and dowsing rods.

- Star anise seeds can be burned to increase psychic powers, or worn as beads; they also make good pendulums. Place one at each of the four directions on your altar for added power.

- Thyme worn in a sachet aids development of subtle senses and enables you to see fairies.

- Yarrow flowers in tea improve psychic powers.

Everyone has some amount of magical awareness, just as everyone has some physical senses. The key to developing your mystical sensitivity is practice. The more you use your subtle senses, the more powerful and refined they will grow. Do not get discouraged if your perceptions manifest differently than you expected or wanted. Try different exercises until you find some that work for you, and repeat them regularly. Using herbs, stones, and other tools can open new senses, speed your development, and boost the strength of your current senses. In time, you will find that you can perceive the magical as easily as you perceive the mundane!

Recommended Resources

Books

Balcombe, Betty F. (1994). *The Psychic Handbook* (2nd ed.) Originally published in 1988. Samuel Weiser.

Browne, Silvia & Harrison, Lindsay. (2007) *Psychic Children: Revealing the Intuitive Gifts and Hidden Abilities of Boys and Girls.* Dutton Adult.

Huson, Paul. (2001). *How to Test and Develop Your ESP* (2nd ed.) Originally published in 1975. Madison Books.

Morwyn. (1999). *The Complete Book of Psychic Arts.* St. Paul, MN: Llewellyn.

Robinson, L. A. & Carlson Finnerty, L. (2004). *The Complete Idiot's Guide to Psychic Awareness* (2nd ed.). Alpha.

Internet Resources

Faerie K. (n.d). "Visualizing by Ear (And Some Other Senses Too)" Originally published in Finnish in Vox Paganorum, January 2002, translated from the Finnish by Faerie K. Retrieved July 9, 2007, from http://www.ecauldron.com/vizbyear.php.

"Second Sight" (2007). Retrieved from http://en.wikipedia.org/wiki/Second_sight.

Wulf, Companion. (2006). "The Clair Senses." Retrieved from http://ferewulf.freehostia.com/clairsenses.htm.

Elizabeth Barrette *serves as the managing editor of* PanGaia Magazine *and assistant editor of* SageWoman Magazine. *She has been involved with the pagan community for more than sixteen years, and in 2003 earned ordination as a priestess through Sanctuary of the Silver Moon. She lives in central Illinois and enjoys herbal landscaping and gardening for wildlife.*

Illustrations: Kyle Fite

Creating Sacred Space

Lisa McSherry

Sacred space has no limitations; it can be as small as the breath taken in a prayer, as elaborate as a cathedral, as expansive as an ocean shoreline. The very act of creating sacred space makes us spiritually receptive to the sacred, as well as gives us a specific place to pray or meditate or perform rituals. Creating an altar gives you a place to find what connects your heart to the larger heart of the universe.

Building altars—personal places of prayer, ritual, and meditation—is one way to acknowledge the holiness of the space we inhabit. When we acknowledge that something greater than ourselves

Creating an altar begins with the process of articulating thoughts and feelings about the sacred in a physical way, and bringing those thoughts and feelings into full consciousness.
LISA MCSHERRY

exists, we create an environment where a sense of the sacred can be realized in us and in the details of our everyday lives. Altars don't "make" space sacred; they show us what has been there all along; they release energy within us and around us that we were not aware of. In a sense, they help us refocus our spiritual eyesight by providing visual clues to help us center and retreat from the distractions of daily life.

The tradition of setting aside an inviolable area for the holy transcends cultures. The Chinese built an altar in their homes and offered food and incense daily to the ancestors, whom they believed to be benevolently watching over the family and guiding it to prosperity. In Japan, where living space is scarce, craftsmen created the step *tansu* (chest) to place in the space under a staircase. And many Hindu households contain a shrine at which daily meditation, singing, and chanting occurs.

Household altars are often elaborate works of art, surrounded by sumptuous wall hangings of embroidery and detailed, colorful paintings. They may have deity images made from precious stone, or covered in gold. Not all altars need be works of art, however. An altar's beauty lies within the intention of the person(s) who builds it. An altar resonates with a feeling of wholeness that transcends place and time and helps provide continuity and richness in all aspects of life; it can be as simple or elaborate as the creator wishes.

Intention

You can't set up a personal altar a "wrong" way. The deity doesn't care whether the altar is perfect or not; its perfection is in the eye of the altar-maker. What differentiates an altar from a simple grouping of objects on a table or mantle piece is intention. What begins as a collection of meaningful objects ends up quite different when a we tap into why we are placing them in a particular relationship to one another.

We often organize our homes according to how they will look and by what things mean to us. Take a moment to think about it, and you will probably realize that certain objects or places in your home make you feel more comfortable or energetic or more in touch with yourself. That may be where you want to begin. Building an altar is the next step to awareness.

Creating Sacred Space

Sacred space can be created in any room, regardless of the size or location. It is as simple as understanding the power existent in the five basic elements: Earth, Fire, Air, Water, and Spirit.

BEGIN WITH THE ELEMENT EARTH

Earth represents the foundation: it's our base stability. You'll want to clean the environment before you use it by first vacuuming, scrubbing, tidying-up—whatever needs to be done. You're actually purifying the space and removing any negative energies inherent in clutter or dirt that can indicate disorder rather than an environment under your control.

ADD FIRE

Candles are basic in sacred space. Use white candles for peace and purity, or use candles created with color of intent as you would in ritual. For instance, purple symbolizes power and ambition, while green is for finance and luck. The energy within your space is affected by color choice, just as in candle magick, and white is always safe.

Add Air

Open a window or a door, or turn on a fan. A light breeze is best but machine-produced air circulation is very adequate. Burn a purifying incense, scented candles, or heat-scented oil.

Add Water

As in ritual, bathing before entering your space will enhance your experience. Goblets or crystal bowls filled with water can be placed about the room. (This also has a mild humidifying effect.) Depending on your finances and creativity, you could place a miniature water fountain in the room or a picture of the sea.

Finally, Add Spirit

You might begin with representations of favored deities—the Virgin Mary, Athena, Pan, Apollo, etc. Then, compose yourself, get comfortable, and be in the moment. Explore the divine within yourself and see where it takes you.

Creating an Altar

The act of creating an altar begins the process of articulating thoughts and feelings about the sacred in a physical way, and bringing those thoughts and feelings into full consciousness. We use many words to describe altars. Words like energy, direction, and meaning refer to the process of seeking the self; while peacefulness, calm, and strength address a state of mind. Usually, there are words that connect to finding the sacred in daily life. The words prayer, meditation, and communication, for example, help us to focus on something larger than the self and the day to day. Creating an altar is not like decorating; it's a search for meaning or a process of discovering what has meaning for you.

Available space and convenience will be primary factors in determining where to place an altar. Many people choose the room or area in their home where they spend the most time in. Some people believe it should be visible from the bed, which is a safe haven for thought and quiet. Still

others believe an altar should be placed wherever the energy is needed. No room is inappropriate for creating sacred space—not even the bathroom. (If you have small children that might be the only place you can find peace for a few minutes!)

How to orient your altar is also a matter of personal choice. The simplest method is to orient the altar according to the four directions (or cardinal points). Many people like that approach because it links interior sacred space to the natural world outside, as well as to the sun, the moon, and the stars. Different cultures associate different qualities with the four directions and many people also choose to ascribe personal meanings to them. There are no hard and fast rules about this.

The Cardinal Points

The six cardinal points are North, South, East, West, the Sky (up), and the Earth (down). The cardinal points (directions) are also linked to the Native American medicine wheel, which is another possible guide to placing and orienting your altar.

The Medicine Wheel

The medicine wheel in its earliest form was probably a simple circle of stones set into the earth, which represented the wheel of life that sits below Father Sky and on Mother Earth. What is most important in Native American thought is that there is no distinction between the sacred and the profane—the universe is animated by supernatural principles that are interconnected and in harmony. The role of ritual is to bring the individual or tribe into harmony with the wheel of life.

Different tribes associate different totemic animals and birds with the directions, as well as colors, gemstones, vegetation, and deities. In the tradition of the medicine wheel, the four directions can be understood as follows:

East

As the direction of the dawn, East is also the place of enlightenment and new knowledge. An altar facing east will draw on burgeoning power. East is also the direction of spring and growth, birth and childhood; its color is yellow, its stone amber, and its totemic animal is the golden eagle.

West

As the place of the setting sun and the moment between day and night, West is the direction of contemplation. It is associated with the autumn, which lies between summer and winter; it's the place both of harvest and of letting go, and the direction we face when we are ready to begin the journey into self-discovery. Its colors are the deepest of browns and black, its stone is obsidian, and its totemic animal is the bear or, sometimes, the raven.

South

As the place of the high-in-the-sky sun and the lush growth of summer, the South is the direction of activity and productivity. It's an empowering direction to maximize the energy you need to follow an already chosen path. Its colors are red and, sometimes, green; its stone is red, and its totemic animal is the coyote.

North

As the place of crystal clarity and of the winter sky, North is the direction of internalization and quiet; it's the place where we burrow deep beneath the frozen ground of the self and come back up with true self-knowledge and wisdom. Make an altar facing north to begin a journey of self-discovery. Its color is white, its stone is the crystal, and its totemic animal is the white owl.

ALTARS FOR SPECIAL PURPOSES

Altars can be built to celebrate or mark turning points in life, to help heal grief or pain, or simply to focus energy on a specific part of life that needs attention. They can provide focus and calm in an unsettled or otherwise distracting situation.

Workplace Altars

It's a good idea to decide beforehand whether you want to answer a colleague's questions about your altar. You may decide that you want your workplace altar to blend into its surroundings. Begin by looking at the area in which you work. What direction do you face? What do you look at? Does the place promote or inhibit productivity? Treat the space as if it matters to you and neaten it by filing or throwing out papers you don't need, dusting, and so on.

Then, choose the place for your altar based on your needs. You may want to pick a spot where you can rest your eyes and your spirit during the workday. If you work in an office with a window, using your window as an altar is a nice option. The simple addition of a few fresh flowers, particularly scented ones, will raise your spirits and energy, and provide a focal point for a moment of quiet during the bustle of the day. Natural objects—a shell or a small crystal—can act as visual reminders of the natural world outside the ebb and flow of all things, including the occasional work-related crisis. Sacred imagery—a statue of Athena for invention or an image of a wolf for leadership—can be used to help you maximize your strengths. Other images—a Kuan Yin goddess statue for compassion or a snake for energy and transformation—can keep you focused on qualities you strive to incorporate into your working day. (I use a small bronze statue of Ganesh to help me clear away obstacles.)

If your job requires that you work closely with other people, try building an altar that supports partnership, choosing pairs of objects or a symbol—such as a knot, to signify interdependence—along with images of fruition. Try working with color on your altar to change the energy level. Choose brightly colored objects for high energy, and softer colors for a calming effect.

Carving out a bit of sacred space in the office, no matter how small or unobtrusive, is an important reminder that the various dualisms our society encourages us to believe in (the separation of the sacred and profane, the intellect and the spirit, the mind and body, the professional and the personal) are really not helpful if we intend to live productive, fulfilled, and spiritually rewarding lives. By creating sacred space where we work, we signify our presence there and our intention to use the time we spend at work as fruitfully as possible.

Portable Altars

A portable or traveling altar can be simply a print or a small-scale statue, a few stones or a crystal, or a small piece of cloth. The human impulse to create meaningful space, to make ourselves spiritually and emotionally at home wherever we are, sometimes reveals itself long before we are conscious of the true meaning of those actions. Creating sacred space helps center and ground us, reminding us of who we are, no matter where we are.

A friend of mine was leaving America to begin a series of jobs overseas and he asked me to create a portable altar for him. I found a wooden box, about 8″ x 8″ x 6″, with a sliding top. Inside, I put a white votive candle, a small box of stick incense, a vial of sea salt, a small ceramic dish, a feather, a silk scarf, and a few items with special meaning for him. It all fit perfectly and was quite unobtrusive in appearance. He has since told me (several times) how perfect it is, and how grounded he continues to feel despite being far away from home.

Outdoor Altars

If you are lucky enough to have private space outdoors, then consider creating an altar (or several) there.

An altar made of earth is an ongoing dedication to the equinoxes. These can be built in the forest or field, or right in your yard. They can be any shape, but the most common is of a serpent winding its way toward a giant egg. The important thing to remember when building an earthwork altar is to take pleasure in it, to feel the earth as you mold your altar into a shape. You may then plant seeds or seedling plants, or just leave it bare.

Garden altars are living altars that bridge nature by nurturing; they are a wonderful way to celebrate nature itself. If possible, set your garden altar near trees and plant flowers that will attract birds, butterflies, and such. If you like to attract butterflies, plant daisies, salvia, globe amaranth, and lupine. Many birds are fond of sunflowers, millet, and coreopsis; and hummingbirds like jasmine and honeysuckle. Place a bird bath on or near the altar and remember to place a few stones in it so that the butterflies may sip from the water, too.

For millennia, trees were the first altars as well as guardians for the people. Trees reach from their roots in the underworld up to the vastness of the sky, and symbolize the life force. Simple offerings such as a flower planted at the base of a tree, a stone circle, a crystal, or a written prayer can be hung from the tree.

Ancestor Altars

This altar is set up to honor those members of the family who are now in the Otherworld, as well as close friends or teachers who have helped you along the way. An ancestor altar can also include historical people, someone whom you might admire or feel a past-life connection to, and spirit guides.

Astral Altars

Most altars are physical things, but an astral altar can be made by using visualization. The astral altar is created in meditation and it has no external components. Some people think that to have a proper altar requires very specific physical things, and that if they do not have access to those things, they cannot make use of the altar. But if you remember that you can build an astral altar, you need never be dependent on external tools.

• • • • • • • • • • • • •

Maintaining sacred space requires your attention. Spend time there daily. Drink a cup of tea and think of nothing. Journal. Meditate. If nothing else, read an uplifting book! The more time you spend in your sacred space, the more often you bring your attention to the space, the simpler it will be for you to slip into a sacred state of mind. After a while, simply being there will help remind you of what is sacred in your life.

Lisa McSherry's *complete bio can be found on page 107.*

Illustrations: Rik Olson

A Book of Shadows

Gail Wood

I work in a small, traditional, and con-servative community; it's picturesque and beautiful, full of beautiful old houses and churches. In the summer-time, every church has a sign announc-ing their Vacation Bible School (VBS). Usually, VBSs have a fun and clever theme like fiesta, space exploration, or sailing. My fun-loving grandmother taught VBS, and I have fond memories of going there one year.

Each morning, for five days, we gath-ered in the church community build-ing. We didn't have to dress up in hot, scratchy church clothes; we got to wear our play clothes. The formality of church was gone. We'd sing songs, play a game, and then do a fun craft. Often, the activities were centered around a Bible story or verse but we weren't beat over the head with it. Just before noon, we'd end the time there with a song and a snack. For years and years, my mother kept the plaques my brother and I painted during that VBS.

A few years ago, I attended a pagan festival which included a witch and wizard school for the children who came. Each day the children would gather in an open-air tent, sing pagan songs, do some kind of craft, and end with snacks. Throughout the festival, we'd see children with the craft they created, dressed in their witch and wizard play clothes. They'd be casting spells and sharing what they learned with everyone who would listen. It was adorable, and probably more fun than some of the adult workshops.

· · · · · · · · · · · ·

So, I'm driving to and from work, all the while looking at the VBS signs, remembering the witch and wizard school, and feeling wistful about those summer days of childhood freedom and play. I wondered, *why should kids have all the fun?* Then, I realized that as a magical person I could make my desires manifest and I could have that kind of summer fun usually reserved for children! Moreover, as an adult and a magical worker, I am not tied to time and place. I could have my five days of fun and craft throughout the summer, even at night! Plus my friends and fellow witches could join me. My plan kept expanding. If my friends couldn't attend, then I could have my power animals, my patron gods and goddesses, as well as the connection to the devas and spirits—all in this world.

Vacation Book-of-Shadow School
for Grown-up Witches

I developed a flexible, moveable Vacation Book-of-Shadow School for Grown-up Witches (VBSGuW). The rules are few but important.

Rules for Play

- The word *workshop* is not allowed; and work is not allowed because this is play.

- Have fun. Do things you like to do.

- Feel free to change my suggestions into an event that will be enjoyable for you.

- This VBSGuW is designed for a group or for an individual working with the spirits of the sacred world. After all, we are never truly alone because we are all connected to this world and the other worlds. Whatever you choose is perfect for you.

- Wear play clothes. This can mean shorts and a T-shirt, pagan garb, or skyclad. It's completely your choice. Be comfortable and happy in your choice of clothing—you don't even have to lay them out the night before if you don't want to.

- Gather together all the things you need for your VBSGuW ahead of time so that you aren't rushing around during your playtime.

- Be messy and enjoy it! Part of the fun of crafts and the Craft is the mess. You will need aprons, gloves, newspapers, and the other things needed to protect your body, clothing, furniture, and floors, because we are still smart even in our play.

- Create an altar for each session. It doesn't matter if it is simple or elaborate as long as it's part of your playtime.

- Plan the time to correspond with your natural rhythms and preferences. If you're not a morning person, have your play-time at night.

Gathering

Each day of VBSGuW is about three hours long; a time frame long enough to relax and have a happy time but not so long that it impinges deeply on the rest of your busy life. Think of it as a positive time-out to connect with your inner witchling. Begin each session in a similar fashion by chilling out, telling jokes, and sharing your lives. Then, distinctively separate into your magical gathering by casting a flexible circle. Call in the spirits that guide you and are a part of your life. Sing, dance, chant, and have fun. End with a snack—some kind of special cakes and ale. Then say goodbye to each other with hugs and the traditional farewell:

> *The circle is open but unbroken.*
> *Merry have we met, merry may we part*
> *and merry may we meet again.*

VBSGuW Day by Day

The inspiration for the VBSGuW comes from the sacred world, the gods and goddess that speak to your inner divinity and inner witchling. While we don't need to have these sessions on the exact day of the week, we will take our divine inspiration from the days of the week: Monday, Tuesday, Wednesday, Thursday, and Friday. In English, each day is named after an Anglo-Saxon god or goddess. Others followed suit and named their days after corresponding goddesses and gods.

MONDAY

Monday (or Moonday) takes its name from the Anglo-Saxon word for moon and honors the goddess of the moon (in modern days, all the goddesses of the moon). A good time for this play day is on or near the full moon. To celebrate this "moon day," we will be making a full moon reflecting pool. It can be large to fill a back yard space or small to fill a balcony or window sill. It depends on the size of the objects you make. After the full moon reflecting pool is complete, you can use it to reflect the moon and draw down the wisdom of the Goddess.

The supplies you will need are a small silver mixing bowl, a clay flower pot into which the bowl will fit, colored clay, soil, glitter, paints, cookie cutters, brushes, and other craft supplies. If you can't find a silver mixing bowl, use a small glass bowl painted silver with oil-based enamel paint.

To make your full moon reflecting pool, you will be "planting" the bowl in your clay pot. Begin by painting your clay pot in colors you like and decorate it with images of the Goddess and the moon. Make it a beautiful tribute to the moon and to the Goddess. Suspend judgment and enjoy the process and the wonderful product of your work. When you are done and the pot is sufficiently dried, you are ready to "plant" the pool.

Fill the pot with enough soil so that you can put the bowl in the pot and the edge of the bowl is level with the rim of the pot. Place the bowl in the pot and fill in the empty spaces with the remaining soil. Make sure that the bowl is planted in such a way that you can remove it and then return it to its place. Decorate the landscape around your pool with shapes you make out of clay. Cookie cutters are good for creating shapes and objects; paint them and use glitter and other shiny things. Create stars, goddesses, spirals, animals and other objects. Don't be concerned with making it good enough, concentrate on having a fun time. Place your clay objects around your reflecting pool.

When you are happy with your reflecting pool, place all of the objects on the altar. With song and chant, raise a cone of power to consecrate this reflecting pool:

> *Goddess of the moon reflect your love,*
> *Goddess of the moon, reflect your joy,*
> *Show your wisdom in this pool.*

Chant and move until the power moves into the universe with a whoosh! End your playtime with a snack.

At the full moon as the moon is rising, fill the garden pool with water. You might want to put a shell in the bottom to further enhance the feminine goddess energy. Cast your circle and place the garden in your circle so that the moon is reflected in the water. Breathe deeply and ask the radiant moon goddess to share her wisdom with you and through you. Open your heart and your soul and hear the wisdom of the moon. When you are finished, open your circle and return the water to the earth with gratitude.

Tuesday

Tuesday is named for the Norse god Tyr, who predated Odin and was the god of justice. It takes discernment and wisdom to understand the pleas for justice and fairness and sometimes this need for justice asks us to look into our own darkness. So on this day, to see truly in both the light and the dark, we will be making a black scrying mirror. The black surface of the mirror invites us to explore the depths of a question so that when we emerge, we are better able to discern what is fair and compassionate to ourselves and others.

Making the mirror is fun and messy. You will need a glass, oil-based black enamel paint, and all the supplies that go along with painting, including the brushes, clothes, newspapers, and clean-up solvent. A picture frame with a glass insert is an ideal choice for a scrying mirror.

Paint the back side of the glass. You may need several coats, letting it dry between coats. During this process, laugh and talk about your experiences with divination and seeking the wisdom of the light and dark. Sing songs and chants. Ask the Goddess for wisdom and compassion. When the painting is done and dried, place the mirror into the frame, with the darkened side to the back of the frame. Take some time to decorate the frame around your new scrying mirror. Be sure to leave a large space of darkness so when you scry, you are not distracted by the decorations.

Place the scrying mirrors on the playtime altar and ask the gods and goddesses of wisdom, compassion, and justice to bless your mirror. Surrounding the mirrors with tarot cards such as Justice, Temperance, the World, Judgment, and the Fool helps to lend very old divination energy to your new scrying tool. Chant and sing the following:

Mirror, mirror, black as night,
Show us the wisdom and the right.

Sing and chant until you raise a cone of energy. Then, send it into the universe with a whoosh! End your playtime with cakes and ale.

WEDNESDAY

Wednesday is named in honor of Wodan or Odin, the chief divinity of the Norse pantheon and the god of war, death, poetry, and wisdom. According to legend, Odin's weapon, a magical spear he named Gungnir, never missed its target and it always returned to his hand. Today, it is often hard to come to terms with the pairing of war with poetry and wisdom. Aggression is a difficult quality to accept, especially since we are doing this in playtime. But we emphasize the protection aspect of the warrior spirit and combine it with wisdom and creativity. Often when we create something, it is a death of something else. In our case, it is the death of self-judgment and defeat!

In our playtime we will make a wand, one that directs our power and will to a purpose. Not just any wand, but one with a name, and we will imbue it with special qualities. For instance, when I wanted a wand that would assist my communication with animal spirits in other realms, I decorated a wand with animal images, tracks, feathers, bits of bone, and fur. I named it "Creature Talk" and use it during my shamanic journey work.

So find a stick of a size that you hold easily in your hand, that is fairly thin, and 12 to 18 inches long. Be guided by your inner wisdom and resonance. Bring together crystals, stones, feathers, ribbons, thread, and other items to add to your wand. You will also need paint, glue, and other decorative items. In your sacred playtime space, create your wand. You may want to leave some of the bark, strip some off, or remove all of it. As you work, talk about the qualities you want the wand to evoke for you. Paint, draw, or carve the symbols that will mean something to your purpose. Stay focused on the purpose but allow new revelations, including the name for your wand, to emerge as you work.

When everyone is done, stand around the altar and have each person introduce their wand to the group. As each wand is placed on the altar, greet it with "Hail and welcome!" Then chant and sing, and clap as you chant the name of your wand to create a cone of power that whooshes into the universe for the purpose you stated. End your playtime with a snack.

THURSDAY

Thursday is named after Thor, the Norse god of thunder. The noise of thunder often scares away the things that may harm us or intend us ill. During this playtime, we will make a Witches' Bottle. In earlier times, Witches' Bottles were made to scare off witches and protect the house in which the bottle sat. The bottles were placed in windows and entryways to repel those who intended evil. Today's witches have claimed the bottles not to repel witches but to protect them. The traditional bottle contained sharp and bent objects such as pins, nails, tangled thread, and other objects intended to repel, confuse and stop those who intended harm. Some traditional recipes included a written charm and still others contained the urine of the owner of the house. For the latter, I will leave that decision up to you.

Find a jar and then gather together thread, pins, needles, nails and other similar objects. If you know someone who knits or quilts, ask them for their thread snips, used needles, and other objects. They are sure to have them. Old scissors that no longer serve their purpose make a great addition to a witch bottle (to cut through the evil intention of an intruder). Also have some parchment paper, rubber stamps, glue, and fabric on hand.

To create a Witches' Bottle, you mix your intentions in with the objects you use. Place the jar in front of you and as you add the objects, say what it is you wish the object to do. For thread snips and pieces of yarn, you might say, "Tangle the mind of those who do harm so they do not see my house." For a bent pin, you might say, "Point their mind away from me," and so on. This doesn't have to be an ugly thing so be sure to include the prospect of welcoming those who intend good. For a piece of pink yarn, you might say, "Allow only those with affection in their heart to cross my threshold." When you are finished filling the bottle with objects, write a charm such as:

Evil walk away, goodness come in and stay.
Tangle in and tangle out,
Upside down and round-about.
Ill intention find confusion,
Tangle in and tangle out,
Tangle out and tangle in.
Love and joy enter in profusion,
Tangle out and tangle in.
Evil walk away, goodness come in and stay.
As I will it, please make it so
For the good of all and the harm of none.
So mote it be!

Place the charm in the bottle. Seal the bottle lid. Cut out a piece of paper the size of the lid and glue it to the top. Write on the paper: Protected by _____, (insert the protective deity of your choice). I use Medusa and I have a rubber stamp with her image that I stamp right on the bottle top label. You can also make a cloth covering for your Witches' Bottle if you choose.

When everyone is finished, place the bottles on the altar and chant your charm until you raise a cone of power. Feel the energy whoosh into the universe for the protection of all who live in your home. End your playtime with a snack. Place the Witches' Bottle near an entryway or window of your home.

FRIDAY

Friday is dedicated to the goddess Frigg and all goddesses of love, passion, and beauty. This activity offers a perfect way to end the week and prepare for the weekend with a time of pampering and beauty! Bring together things that smell good, feel good, and are luxurious to the senses—incense, essential oils, lotions, polishes, body glitter, and so forth.

This playtime is for beauty; for us to remember that as divine creatures we are beautiful and deserve to have pleasant and wonderful things available to us. In this playtime, we will not be doing or making anything but rather exploring our "be-ing." As I often say, we are not human doings, we are humans be-ing. In deference to a day dedicated to love and beauty, we will be beauty.

In honor of ourselves and each other, we will be washing each other's feet. It is a sensual experience for both the bather and the bathed, so be sure to do both. This is a ritual honoring you both.

Fill a basin with hot water and sweet-smelling soapy suds. Suspend any feelings you might have about worthiness, or worry about whether the other person is comfortable or not. Let go of your self-consciousness and focus on your own experience and pleasure. It is good and it honors you both as the giver and as the receiver.

As you bath someone else's feet, feel the wonderful feeling of the water and the warmth of the soapy liquid. Feel your hands caress the other's feet and draw pleasure in the feeling of water and soap on skin. While you are having your feet bathed, breathe deeply and feel the water on your skin and the hands caressing you. Feel the slippery warmth of the suds.

And when you are done, thank your friends and end your playtime with a delicious snack. Toast each other and thank the spirits for your Vacation Book of Shadows School for Grown-up Witches. You have proven that all the fun is not reserved just for kids, but for real grown-up witches, too.

Gail Wood *started her writing career early when a story she wrote in the first grade was posted on the board by her teacher. The story was about Jo-Jo the monkey. Her mother saved that story for Gail! She is the author of* Rituals of the Dark Moon: 13 Rites for a Magical Path *published by Llewellyn in 2001. Currently, she lives in a 100+ year-old house with her partner Mike and their two dogs. Mike shares her spiritual interests and is an exceptionally fine priest, following the ecstatic path of Gaia.*

Illustrations: Tim Foley

Air, Fire, Water, Earth & Spirit Power

Luna

Meditation is a strong tool with which to connect and bond with the elements. However, not everyone is adept at reaching deep meditative states that facilitate that connection and bonding. If you are unable to attain deep meditative states, there are other avenues that can be explored with equal success. These other avenues also serve to awaken and unlock the creative and artistic abilities.

When I first began actively walking my path, I felt a pull toward the elements. I wanted to embrace and incorporate them in my workings, but twenty years ago, scant little was available in the mainstream world that I could rely upon and use to build a strong spiritual foundation. I considered how the elements would unfold and be revealed to me in my workings and it was not long before I realized that I was as much a part of each element as each element was a part of me.

I began to outline my own course of study and rather than become so overwhelmed with the task of learning the aspects of the elements all at once, I decided to invite them into my life, to learn each element intimately, and to make a connection with each element and embrace it fully as I incorporated it into my path and traveled down my own road to spiritual evolution. What follows is a glimpse into my journey.

Air

Around midsummer, the element of Air becomes dominant in my life. I explore the symbols that represent Air in my life and the themes that suddenly appear, as if by magic, in the world that surrounds me. My awareness of air really started at yoga classes, where breathing is the most important aspect of stilling the mind and readying the body for postures. I learned how to breathe, how to take air into my lungs from outside of my body. I allowed air to change colors as it entered my nostrils, passed through my lungs, circulated through my respiratory system, and left through my mouth. I began to breathe deliberately and I noticed a subtle difference in my perception of Air. I began to feel its life.

I sat on a beach one windy day and watched blowing sand erase the deep footsteps of joggers and passers by, and sailboats sail quickly out of my view. I felt the wind that pushed across cresting waves, sending them crashing into shore and against rocks. I felt the strength of Air.

As summer gave way to fall, I watched the wind blow leaves into circles, whirling with the laughter of children chasing each other and romping through piles of leaves melding with the wind. The air changed from the heat of summer to a hint of chill in the fall. A feeling of happiness played in the wind and whipped my hair every where. I felt its truth.

Fire

I felt apprehensive about working with the element of Fire and its energies. I could feel Air and not be harmed, but the thought of feeling Fire frightened me. I began by taking note of the symbols and representations that fire has in the world. At Mabon, I lit a bonfire and watched flames of fire send brilliant sparks upward into the darkened sky. I remembered how fire crackled and hissed as its energies mixed with air. I remembered Beltane, when drummers surrounded the balefires and beat rhythmically while dancers undulated around the fires of fertility for fields and for wombs, as well as creativity and ideas. I realized that fire helps us realize passion and it warms us to the feeling of that passion.

In the fall, I sought the warmth of a fire in the fireplace, lit to stave off the chill in New England. I readied myself for the death of the Sun King and realized that his warmth was Fire in my soul that would carry me through the long winter. At Yule, I used the last bit of the previous year's Yule Log to light the new Yule Log. The

smell of the fire as it touched the old Yule Log was welcoming and it brought a certain comfort and peace. The warmth of the element Fire stirred within me.

I realized that if I could embrace Fire and make it a part of my spiritual evolution, my journey would be filled with much positive abundance. I envisioned everything negative in my life and I decided that Fire would be the vehicle for positive change that I required. As I began working more intimately with this element, I came to understand that the fear I initially had was not for the element of Fire, but for my own fear of success.

In order to move forward, I incorporated fire into my ritual. I made Fire the vehicle to bring about the fertility of my own fields and of my own creative processes and ideas. I wrote down everything in my life that was negative, or that I wanted to be rid of, and I invited the element of Fire into my workings. I lit a large bonfire and page by page, I invited the flames to carry every one of the negative aspects out of my life and to replace the negativity with the passion of Fire.

I made this ritual my ceremony of Fire and Release, and as I watched the flames consume the slips of paper that contained the negative aspects of my life and carry them onto the wind and out of my life, Fire brought the realization that there is passion in its energies and it warmed me to the feeling of that passion. At Imbolc, I paid homage to the goddess Brigid, and requested her blessings upon my home and family. I gathered candles and placed them around the fireplace, on the hearth, and throughout my home. Fire provides comfort for my family during the cold winter and as the flames flicker and dance, my soul is warmed by the fires of the season.

Water

At Ostara, when fields are being readied for planting and seeds are being sown, I reflect on the nourishment of the soil and the seeds. Water brings nourishment and causes growth to occur. I found myself reflecting more on the nourishment of the soil and the seeds, not only in the fields, but also in my life and in my spiritual journey. I began to concentrate on the aspects of water that cleanse and nourish and that would bring bountiful harvests in the months ahead. I realized that I needed to explore the strength in the element of Water. Being the elixir of life, it plays a vital role in the bounty of the harvest from Lammas to Samhain and I searched for the comparison of the crops to my own journey. I knew then that my spiritual evolution had been suffering from a real drought and it would be the element of Water that would cleanse and nourish me back to spiritual good health.

In the months after Ostara, and at Samhain, when the turning of the wheel begins another pagan year, I reflected on my own harvest. I realized that I was spiritually thirsty. I found myself seeking constant communion with Water. I would walk to the lake and sit in quiet contemplation as water gently rippled away from the shoreline. I watched the drought of summer cause the lake level to drop significantly. It was in that moment that I realized how my own life had suffered a spiritual drought.

Today, I know that the seeds I planted have been nourished by Water and have grown, and that my fields have been cleansed and purified with Water. I take the time to be thankful for the ebb and flow of abundance, learning and growth that have transpired in my life. Like water, I travel a path of least resistance and fill every aspect of my path with life, with positive abundance, and with honor. There is strength in water, yet there is also a peaceful calm in knowing that all life emerges and is sustained by water.

Earth

Earth is an element about which I find myself constantly thinking and feeling. I am an avid gardener and my world revolves around what I am planting, when I will be planting it, where I will be planting it, and how I will be planting it. Ideas, thoughts, projects, spells, and everything else in my world are considered "plantings" and, therefore, my life has many earthy aspects. I look inward at my life and my path as if it were a field, being readied for planting. The element Earth is not just represented by dirt; it's also steadfast continuity, strength, and compassion. It is the core of my existence, the solid foundation upon which my spiritual journey takes place. I see the earth as the dirt under my feet, the wooded mountains in

the distance and the place where the sand meets the sea. I feel the Earth element as the nurturing soil in which I have planted the seed of my soul's evolution.

Spirit

Spirit is the embodiment of each and every other element. Spirit holds them all together and represents them all united as the One True Source and Center, the Great Divine. In each element, in each plant, animal and human, there is Spirit. I cannot look at any living thing and not see the Divine in that entity. Spirit is everywhere, in all things, and is constant. Of all of the elements, Spirit is the most consistent and ever present in all aspects of life.

. . . .

When I had garnered all of my initial experiences of the elements, I realized that simple knowledge of their characteristics was nice but, as a human being, I wanted to embody the essence of the elements and to create something unique to represent each element in my life.

I took photos of the sea, the whirling leaves, birds soaring overhead on the gentle, warm, uplifted breezes, and trees swaying in the wind. I painted a scene with ocean waves crashing against the rocky shore, I painted the autumn foliage on the mountains surrounding the valley, and I painted the balefire in the black night. I took acorns and pinecones from the forest floor, and sand and rocks from the beach. I decorated my sacred space with all of these representations of the aspects and characteristics of the elements as they revealed themselves to me.

Over the years, my relationship with the elements has deepened. I conduct a yearly ritual, usually on the full moon preceding Samhain, to invite each element, in its turn, into my life and I take special care to be thankful for the experiences of each element in my world. Initially, when I used this exercise to create a representation for each element, I realized that I had spent the better part of a year getting acquainted with each element. I realized that this project would be ongoing for the rest of my journey here.

This is an exercise that is ever changing and growing. It brings deeper realization and understanding of the elements into my practice and into my life as each turn of the wheel brings me more in tune with the elements and deepens my spiritual connection. I learned that by feeling the elements and calling them into practice in every aspect of my life, I am more in sync with the world around me. I am traveling my path more directly to fully realize my own spiritual evolution.

Luna *holds a degree in psychology and has been a solitary witch for over twenty years. She is a member of Sacred Flame, a Danbury, Connecticut coven, practicing and celebrating in the Veryus tradition. Luna lives in Sandy Hook, Connecticut, with her devoted husband and their silly dog. She spends her free time gardening, writing, quilting, and making hand-crafted ritual tools. She can be contacted through www.kellisbroomcloset.com.*

Illustrations: Lydia Hess

Roadside Magick

JD Hortwort

Herbs. They are part and parcel of most witches' tool chests. We use them to calm our minds and spirits and to help activate the universe to achieve our goals.

Most cities have at least one herbal store where people can go to purchase herbs. But there is no better way to really connect with the herbs you intend to use than to collect and process your own.

We tend to think of popular herbs like frankincense, mandrake, or sandalwood when we think of herbs. These exotic plants have been used in traditional practice for thousands of years.

The problem is that they are hard to grow in most areas of the U.S. Fortunately, we don't have to travel to far-off lands for our supplies.

Roadside Magick

Look around. In just about any neighborhood in the U.S., you can find plantain for protection, honeysuckle for money and psychic powers, and cherry for love. You just have to look at your environment with new eyes.

GRASS

Step outside your dwelling door. The first thing you will probably see is grass, whether in a well-cut lawn or on the side of the road. Did you realize that grass is used in spells for protection? Just think of the blades you gather as hundreds of little soldiers between you and the danger you perceive.

JUNIPER

Juniper berries—the kind that come from those prickly ground covers, shrubs, and trees that grow in thousands of American landscapes—are also good for protection. Look closely and you'll see small light or dark blue berries clinging to the branches. Pick and use them for protection, exorcism, and health. The common Virginia red cedar that is often seen growing along pasture fences isn't a true cedar. It's a juniper. In summer, watch the branches for tiny blue berries about the size of BB pellets. Gather what you need, but leave plenty for the finches!

TREE LEAVES, WOOD, AND MOSS

Every area of the U.S. abounds with trees that can help you with your magickal pursuits. Gather dogwood leaves or wood for protective

amulets. Maple leaves are used in love spells and for longevity. Of course, the mighty oak conveys protection, health, strength, and prosperity through its bark and acorns. Look closely and you will also find lichen (oak moss) for luck, money, and strength.

DANDELION

Those who live in urban areas shouldn't feel left out. Mother Nature is holding her own along sidewalks, easements, and vacant lots. The humble dandelion plant is a treasure trove. Its root is used for health, calling spirits, and psychic powers. Don't forget to gather the seed head for a quick wish.

CHICORY

In the heat of summer—in the driest conditions—you can find another hardy survivor, the chicory plant. It stands out early in the day with sky-blue flowers held over ragged, toothed leaves. Gather the root to help remove obstacles in your path.

MILKWEED AND MAYAPPLE

Ditches will be home to milkweed in many areas. Butterflies love milkweed and so do fairies. If conditions are right, you may also find the American mandrake, or mayapple. Both are useful in money and love. Poke is frequently found in "waste" areas, but don't let it go to waste. Use the root to break hexes or curses and the berries to create your own magickal ink.

How to Get Started

So many herbs! You just need to get started. First, find some good reference books that will detail what herbs to use for your particular purpose. Good resources will indicate whether you need the leaf, flower, seed, wood, or root. Such resources will also tell you when to gather the herb for greatest effect, whether in a waxing or waning moon, and the proper planetary hour.

To learn about the various plants in your area, contact your local cooperative extension office. The experts there can refer you to books and Internet resources with good color pictures. Don't forget to ask about the "weeds." What the general public refers to as weeds, we pagans consider working resources! Once you have your magickal and mundane library, it's just a matter of cross-referencing.

Traditional herbs are a boon to any magickal practitioner, but little compares to the satisfaction of sourcing and collecting your own herbs. Plus, it lends to the spell because as you gather the plant material, you should be focused on your intent as well. The same old neighborhood is now a brand new world of opportunity. Open your eyes, open your door, and step out into the world of roadside magick!

Some Precautions

In our Western society, all property "belongs" to somebody. You may believe in your heart that no one can own a piece of Mother Earth, but the local authorities will tend to disagree with you. Area governments control easements along roads. The property along the railroad tracks belongs to some railroad company. Even the lot that seems to be abandoned belongs to somebody. While no one is

likely to complain if you gather a dandelion from the crack in the sidewalk, property owners will probably get upset if you show up with a pair of pruners and start lopping branches off a tree on that open lot. The same is true of public areas like neighborhood parks or arboretums. Get permission before you gather, or be prepared to pay the consequences!

Did you realize that utility easements belong to private property owners? Many folks think these areas are abandoned or owned by an absentee utility company that only shows up once a year for maintenance. They are not. Private-property owners give utilities permission to access transmission lines that run across their property for the public good and in exchange for a promise to do property maintenance. Be certain you have permission to be there.

Next, you must remember that, for you, herbs are a tool to supplement magick. For the area wildlife, herbs are food and shelter. Be certain that you collect no more than you need.

Another important consideration is pollution. Roadside herbs should be used in incense or gris-gris bags. Do not eat them or smoke them or drink an infusion from them. When gathering plants away from your home and beyond your control, you will have no idea what as been applied to or absorbed by the plant. Do not ingest them in any form.

Finally, take into consideration the potential for allergies. You might be allergic to mulberries, for example. You will definitely have a reaction to poison ivy. Again, don't ingest any of the plants you gather if you don't personally know how you will react to that plant.

JD Hortwort is a former master gardener and perennial nature girl who resides in central North Carolina. A practicing pagan since 2002, she is also the vice chancellor of Greensboro's House of Akasha. The House of Akasha is a Celtic-based church that is open to pagans of all faiths. In addition to being an avid student of herbology and gardening, JD is a professional freelance writer and an award-winning journalist.

Illustrations: Tina Fong

Pet Memorials

Elizabeth Hazel

Many people feel like their pets are their children. We human guardians generally outlive our pets, and have to cope with the loss of different pets over the years. The death of a pet is a very painful event. In my experience, pagans are animal advocates and many bond deeply with pets. Some pets may even become familiars. In recognition of inter-species relationships, a beloved pet's death should be approached with the same seriousness and dignity accorded the death of a human.

In the case of an elderly pet, whose life is waning, the human guardian has time to prepare and make choices. The first decision is whether to bury or cremate. The second decision is whether to have a funeral, which includes an interment, or to hold a memorial service that may take place some days after the pet has died. Another choice that can be made in advance is to ask a priest or priestess to officiate at the funeral/memorial, or to ask a friend with experience in public speaking to be the officiant.

When a pet dies young or suddenly, the bereaved may be too shocked to handle these decisions, and may need guidance from coven members when making these choices.

A ritual for a memorial service should give tribute to the pet's life, acknowledge the death and pain of loss, and finally, release the pet's soul into the afterlife.

Over the years, I've both sent and received pet obituaries. An obituary gives the pet's name, dates of birth and death, tributes to the personality and character of the pet, and may include an invitation to attend a funeral/memorial ritual, with the date, time, and location. It's easiest to e-mail copies to everyone possible, and make a few hard copies to mail to the people who don't have access to e-mail.

Funeral and memorial services tend to go most smoothly when there is a set order for the ritual. Spontaneous, unstructured rituals often leave people either overwhelmed or underwhelmed. In the face of grief, few people can remain focused enough to conduct a ceremony. A planned ritual gives dignity to the proceedings, provides formal closure for the pet's family, circumvents awkward fumbling, and keeps the ritual to a reasonable length of time.

A priest or priestess, coven member, or family friend should act as master of ceremonies or officiant. This individual makes the

opening and closing remarks, introduces speakers, and explains the significance of any poetry or music. Generally, an officiant keeps the ritual on track and cues other participants when it is their turn.

Memorial services may include all or most of the following elements (adapted from *In Memoriam* by Amanda Bennett and Terence Foley). Tailor the ceremony to suit the type and age of pet and the wishes of the family.

1. A welcoming statement, like "Merry meet and blessed be. We form this circle, by Fire, Water, Air, and Earth, to remember (pet's name), who died last week at the age of _____, after a _____." (Insert the correct date and circumstance of death.)

2. The officiant offers a brief bio that mentions aspects of the pet's life and special qualities.

3. Eulogies. Eulogies are thoughtful remarks about the deceased made by close friends and family members. Specific anecdotes are the most meaningful. Keep remarks short—no more than

three to five minutes. People should be asked in advance so they have time to think of something to say. Gentle humor is not out of place in a eulogy, especially if the pet had quirky or amusing behaviors. Laughter eases grief.

4. Musical interlude.

5. The officiant conducts a short ritual.

6. A prayer, poem, or reading by a friend.

7. Summation/closing. The officiant thanks everyone for attending, and directs attendees to any planned activity after the memorial.

If the ritual includes an interment, this should occur during or after the music. Family, coven members, and friends may take turns shoveling soil into the grave.

Coven members should be prepared to offer aid and support, which may include contributing food, candles, music, eulogies, poems, flowers, or writing the ceremony and making copies for participants.

Special Extras

The tolling of bells is an ancient pagan tradition that begins and ends a ritual. Candle-lighting rituals are also traditional. In ancient times, funeral biers were lit with torches because funerals were conducted at night. Participants may carry candles as they approach the memorial site. Pass a flame from person to person, and place the candles around a grave site or memorial statue.

An indoor ceremony may include an altar with photographs and candles.

Another option is to pass around a loaf of bread during the ritual portion of the ceremony. The officiant may say, "We share this bread in memory of _____." A basket of flowers can be passed around, and each person can lay their flower on the grave at the end of the ritual. Rosemary is traditionally the herb of remembrance, and may be sprinkled or planted on a grave. This is a powerful symbol of the soul's release into the afterlife.

A tree or shrub can mark the location of a grave. The hole should be dug before the ritual begins, and the planting done during the musical interlude (with or without a burial). If the memorial takes place in a park or open space, people can pass around a bowl of grass or wildflower seeds to be cast to the winds after the ceremony.

If the deceased pet is a dog, people may invite others to bring their dogs, and after the memorial service take a "memorial dog walk" along the route the family followed with their pet. People may be asked to make contributions to favorite pet shelters in the name of the deceased pet.

Ritual for a Deceased Pet

A ritual for a memorial service should give tribute to the pet's life, acknowledge the death and pain of loss, and finally, release the pet's soul into the afterlife. The rite may offer the departed soul an invitation to return to the family through reincarnation. A sample is provided below; it may be used as it is, or adapted to suit the family. Following the music (and interment or tree planting), the priest, priestess, or officiant says:

By Fire and Water, by Air and Earth,
Be accepted into the gentle arms of the Goddess.
May she protect and cherish your soul in death
As you were loved and cherished in life.
(For an older pet, continue with:)
This pet lived through all the seasons of life.
In the spring, (pet's name) was a puppy (kitten, hatchling),
Full of energy, life, and curiosity,
And growing from day to day.
In the summer, (pet's name) was young,
Exploring, playing, and learning;
Getting underfoot and into forbidden places,
And adapting to the rhythms of the (guardian's name) family.
From the long hot days of summer
To the cool crisp days of fall,

(Pet's name) was a beloved friend and companion,
Secure in love, true of heart, and a loyal partner.
He (she) gave unconditional love
And comfort to his (her) guardian(s),
And marked the milestones of the eightfold path for many years.
One day there was white on (pet's name) muzzle.
He (she) got up more slowly from longer naps.
And fall became winter.
Though your steps were slower
With age, your love became distilled,
More pure, more fine, more precious.
The winter has ended, dear friend;
We now release you to find the spring again.
*May your soul rise and be comforted in the arms of the Goddess.
May the spirits of Fire light your way through death's dark door,
May the spirits of Air accompany your soul's journey with song,
May the spirits of Earth free you from the sands of time,
And may the spirits of Water soothe you in your transition,
And soothe our hearts as we adapt to your absence.
If it is time, may your soul fly free
And glow with the stars in the sky.
If your soul still heeds the call of earthly love,
Rest for a time, and refresh your spirit
in the space between life and the veil that conceals the unknown.
When your spirit is renewed,
You are welcome to return in a new form,
To share love and companionship with your family again.
Their hearts and doors are open to you,
Should you choose to return.
So mote it be, blessed be!

For a younger pet that may have died unexpectedly, begin with:

In the spring, (pet's name) was a baby,
A puppy (kitten, hatchling, etc.) full of energy, life, and curiosity,
Growing from day to day.
In the summer, (pet's name) was young,
Exploring, playing, and learning;
Getting underfoot and into forbidden places,
And adapting to the rhythms of the (guardian's name) family.
Now your life has been cut short,
Denying us the pleasure of sharing our lives with you
And enjoying your companionship.
Our hearts tremble with the loss and pain of your absence,
And we mourn that you will not grow old with us.
(resume at*)

Different branches of neopaganism have different gods and goddesses to whom the soul of the pet may be entrusted. Cats may be given into the charge of Bast, the cat-headed Scorpion goddess Selket (Egyptian); Freya (Norse); Aphrodite, Artemis, or Hecate (Greek). Dogs may be given into the charge of Anubis (Egyptian), Thor or Odhinn (Norse); Ares/Mars, Artemis/Diana, or Hecate (Greek/Roman). Consider the deity with whom your pet has the greatest affinity, and insert the name into this closing summation, which is recited by the officiant:

(Pet's name), you now make your final journey,
From this world into the next.
Thank you for being a blessing for your family,
And for sharing your precious life with us.

We give your body unto Mother Earth,
and commend your spirit to (god/goddess name).
We release you into the spirit world
With prayers for your safe passage and happy resting,
And prayers for a safe return,
Should you choose to come back to us.
Fly now, into the arms of (god/goddess)!
No fear, harm, illness, or injury
Will befall you in his (her) protected realm.
We honor the Great Goddess (or Lord and Lady)
In this sad episode in the cycle of life,
And remember that death is a part of life,
And that all life yields to death.
Be with us, (God / Goddess), and comfort us in our sorrows.
By the four elements,
By the Great Goddess (or Lord and Lady),
By the spark of divinity that is shared by all,
May we be blessed, and blessed be!
So mote it be!

At the conclusion of the ceremony, a friend may cue up some soft background music that will allow everyone a moment to pray, meditate, or cry before sharing a meal, a memorial walk, or some other activity. Sharing a meal gives people a chance to talk about the deceased pet and share memories in a more conversational way, and to decompress from intense emotions.

Coven members should be prepared to offer aid and support, which may include contributing food, candles, music, eulogies, poems, flowers, or writing the ceremony and making copies for participants. They may accompany the bereaved guardian on difficult errands (reclaiming cremains, or purchasing an urn or memorial statue). Coven members may also select a tree if a planting will be part of the memorial.

One memorial is rarely enough to give closure. Indeed, repeat memorial tributes for deceased pets at Samhain, and again a year after death.

I hope this short guide to pet memorials is useful, and I dedicate it to the memory of the cats I've loved and lost. In the truest sense of the phrase, I close with "Merry meet, merry part, and merry meet again"—in this life and the next.

Elizabeth Hazel (Lady Vala Runesinger) *is an astrologer, tarotist, and author of* Tarot Decoded. *She writes various horoscope columns, including* "Astro-Spell" (newWitch Magazine), *and is the editor of the* ATA Quarterly Journal. *Elizabeth's Web site can be found at http://kozmic-kitchen.com.*

Illustrations: Carolyn Vibbert

Magical Transformations

The Star Queen

Calantirniel

I wouldn't discover Varda Elentari, the Star Queen and most beloved of the Valar, until many years later, but I think I searched for her from the time I was a child.

When I was young, I loved nature. I would scoop autumn leaves into a pile, lie on them, and watch the sky—endlessly. And the sky never ceased to amaze me—especially on a clear night. I loved to watch the silvery moon change shapes as it passed through the sky night after night.

In school, I loved to draw stars, all with varying numbers of points, and I

wanted to execute them perfectly. Later, when I would camp with my family, my mother brought a star map so we could identify constellations. The map included a general discussion of the signs in the astrological zodiac. My favorite constellation was the Big Dipper, also called the Great Bear (although I never understood why).

As time passed and I grew older, I put aside my relationship with the natural world and began to focus on people. I discovered that could actually be quite social. Unfortunately, I forgot that no matter how hurried and busy we are, we need to reconnect with the energy of the cycles. Needless to say, I ended up like most people; I was utterly disconnected from nature's cycles. Because I wasn't in the flow at all, I had made some rather unenlightened decisions by the time I was a young adult.

When the negative results of those decisions came to fruition, my extremely sharp and active mind was confused. Because of my linear view of time (thanks to my excellent grasp of the teachings in today's society), I felt ruined. How could I be so fooled if I was as smart as society said I was? I had to figure it out and to make corrections wherever it was possible. At that moment, something new awakened in my consciousness in a most unexpected way— through an attorney who used astrology to win his cases.

The Star Queen

At the time, I was a legal secretary, using all the capacity of my left brain to handle the numerous details of the mundane. Part of me liked performing those challenging duties well, but I also felt like I was utterly dying inside. At the time, I was also a single mom, and a predictable paycheck and job security were important. But that voice of discontent was becoming louder within me; I just couldn't see myself doing the mundane work very much longer, regardless of all the benefits.

When I gave my birth date, time, and place to an attorney I knew, he told me things that he had no way of knowing about me. He then proceeded to tell me things that even I didn't know about me! Because I was almost thirty, I was experiencing a Saturn return (a time when areas of your life, where you have lessons to learn, fall apart).

I devoured every astrology book he had and was fascinated beyond all comprehension. Then, I started collecting my own books and devoured them. The best single thing I learned from astrology is that time is not linear. It happens in cycles, and the planetary motion through the zodiac is a way to measure these cycles.

Years of dedicated study followed. I learned to interpret the cycles and translate them into real experience—for others as well as myself. After a while, as my right brain became more open, even more information came in. It became clear to me that when you are in the flow, you make better decisions, and thereby achieve better outcomes. I also picked up other arts—tarot reading, pendulum dowsing, crystals, aromatherapy, flower essences, reiki—and eventually, I saw how it all fit together for me.

I was already pulling away from the legal field by modeling part time. Inadvertently, I'd also started a business making crocheted

> ... the Star Queen had something up her sleeve that would bewilder all of us. Indeed, another door flew wide open with me sailing on my rear into the other side, and although events foreshadowed it, nothing prepared me for what was to come.

head wear. Both modeling and crocheting are creative (and risky) occupations, but then I also became a professional astrologer. In hindsight, I saw how star energy related to each of these. I even see how star energy was infused into the crochet business: the majority of my hat designs happen to originate with a "sun," which is a star in its own right.

Through the fires of my burning desire to relearn, reclaim, and re-live my star nature, I watched my old life combust, turn into ashes, and blow away. I was reborn—and restored—to my original star-like state. Walking into an office environment today would make me cringe; I just can't do it anymore. When I look back, it seems that someone other than me had those banking and legal secretary jobs.

The Star Queen Makes Her Presence Known

In April 2005, upon my husband's suggestion (and after seeing the *Lord of the Rings* movies), I began reading his crumbling copy of *The Silmarillion* (originally published in 1977), which contained Tolkien's middle-earth "back-stories." Therein, I discovered the elven pantheon, which is called the Valar. I hit the spiritual jackpot with Varda Elentari, the Star Queen—most beloved of the Valar by the Elves (who interestingly are also called the People of the Stars). I had delayed reading this work for a long time because I thought they were just made-up stories, but while I was reading it, I just knew with every cell of my very being that these stories were real —in a mythic mode. Varda's archetypal energies were gener-ated from the deepest primordial wells of our forgotten ancestors' origins, and I felt her come alive inside of me that day!

What was unbelievable to me was the fact that no one else had figured this out, or maybe they had but didn't dare admit it. After all, it does seem rather crazy and illogical. After considerable effort, I did manage to find others who felt the same way.

However, no matter how hard we looked, no spiritual path that sufficiently embodied this mythos seemed to exist. So what else is there to do but make one? During this process, I have read and integrated more of the materials that Tolkien spent fifty-six years of his life perfecting. As I continue to read (and study Quenya, an Elvish language), I feel closer than ever to the Star Queen archetype, and interestingly, I have transformed yet again. And, very likely, I will continue to transform!

Archetypal Exploration

During the time of my transformation, I studied many forms of spirituality, and felt most drawn to those based on nature and an honoring of the cycles through the seasons as well as the stars. Because of my astrological studies, I had a good handle on the Greek and Roman pantheons, and even the Oracle of Delphi has special meaning to me. Because of my strong Celtic, Teutonic, and Native American genetics, I also felt at ease with the ways of the wise-woman, with more emphasis on healing than crafting, and always in the balance of nature and the cycles. I am quite drawn to the Egyptian pantheon and feel very close to Isis, the daughter of the star/sky goddess Nuit. I've studied her for some time, along with her relationships to others of the pantheon. I also find I resonate with Eastern Indian and Vedic principles. To me, the Buddha reaching "enlightenment" totally describes an aspect of the Star Queen's influence.

I found myself wanting to "tune in" more clearly to the Star Queen herself, and discovered a couple of other expressions of her: Astraea in the Greek pantheon, Arianrhod in the Celtic pantheon, Ira of the Polynesian pantheon, and Citlalicue in the Aztec pantheon. All of these, of course, were pieces of the puzzle, and yet I connected with the Egyptian Isis most strongly. My desire was to integrate the Star

Queen within a Celtic/Teutonic practice. I discovered that Victor and Cora Anderson's Feri tradition has the Star Goddess as a central deity figure. Although I really like the energy of fae, I do not feel like a part of it—closer, but no dice.

This time, the Star Queen had something up her sleeve that would bewilder all of us. Indeed, another door flew wide open with me sailing on my rear into the other side, and although events foreshadowed it, nothing prepared me for what was to come. I notice that the Star Queen's influence continues to transform me, leading me now to become an author. Because plants and planets have associations as well, I was also led to become a master herbalist. I can now see how each of these outward "points" of my personal star energy are all centered in and based upon principles of healing. This article in no way is meant to diminish the importance of managing mundane, detailed work—and sometimes the talents I have learned from that world help me greatly. However, if you discover that you resonate with the Star Queen, it becomes clear that your life mission is to serve as a healer, whether you think you will or not!

FINDING YOUR OWN CONNECTION TO THE STAR QUEEN

I hope my story inspires you to seek the Star Queen's expression in your own life. The following are merely suggestions, and you may want to come up with your own ideas of connection, which if you ask me, are the best kind!

Study the Sky

This may seem obvious, but go outside on a clear night to a place where city lights don't cast light into the sky. The stars appear brighter when the moon is new, and when it gets really cold and dry. The atmosphere in these conditions apparently allows the sparkle of the stars to really come through, and the sky is quite a sight—just bundle up! The sky is equally beautiful when the moon is present. A star chart is not necessary, but you may feel inspired to seek one out. They can be found in books, magazines, newspapers, or on the Internet. Say hello to the Star Queen in whatever way feels natural to you. Feel the starlight and/or moonlight pouring down upon you, filling you with healing and wisdom.

And remember that even the daytime sky has the sun, our closest star! It is interesting that though the sun is smaller in size compared to other stars, the closeness allows it to give off so much light that other stars are not visible when the sun is. The sun's warmth and light allows plants to grow, and no matter what foods we consume (the closer to nature, the better), all deliver to us the healing lights of the sun, moon, and stars.

Be Creative: Draw, Paint, Crochet—the Sky Is the Limit!

Drawing stars in many shapes—even into constellation shapes—will help you connect with them. You can also study the numerology of any star by counting its points, and even come up with your own impressions in whatever way you see fit for you. You can easily find information online about the energies of varying numbers of points in any type of star. Don't limit yourself to drawing. You can paint them, or even crochet them. You may also see the relationship with star shapes and many flowers, and using flower essences is an excellent way to explore these energies. Through your experience and research (many plants have planetary rulers), you can relate your impressions to the star shapes, and maybe even to stars in the sky. Allow the Star Queen to guide you.

Study Astronomy

This is a logical follow-up to the first suggestion: study astronomy. Many resources are available, and you can go as shallow or as deep as you like—not to mention, telescopes can be fun! It can be very enlightening to see how the sky changes through the hours, and even through the times of the year. Also, look at what the sky would look like in the opposite hemisphere from where you live. The Southern Hemisphere has a much different star view than the Northern Hemisphere.

Study Astrology

You can learn about the zodiacal signs, constellations, the planets, and the myths behind all of the signs and symbols. There are even mythologies aligned with what is known as the fixed stars. These

mythologies will give you clues as to their meaning and even magical uses.

Make a Wish Upon a Star
This one is fun: make a wish on a star! Just visualize your wish, put it into an imaginary "penny" and "toss" it, seeing it land on your chosen star! I find stars and planets tend to be similar to wishing wells, and they make great familiars. Interestingly, through personal meditation, I have been made aware of the mystical watery nature rather than the logical fiery nature of stars. If you have different impressions, go with your impressions, because the Star Queen may work differently with different individuals.

Meditate
Meditation is an excellent way to connect with the Star Queen. I will share a simple one here for exploring Varda Elentari.

After drinking some water (possibly infused with a favorite flower essence), relax and close your eyes. Visualize being outside on a clear night in the healing silvery lights of Isil, the moon, and Elenillor, the stars. The ever-beautiful Varda appears before you and takes you on a sky journey, showing you many constellations and sharing Elven star lore, including the stories of Anar, the sun, and Valacirca, the Big Dipper, which is in place to keep at bay the unnamed one who only perpetuates negative thoughts and deeds (he is very afraid of her). See and feel the primal light emitting from her, feel her strength and perfect protection. Ask her for her protective coat of light and feel yourself becoming restored and renewed. Before coming back, you get a glimpse of the magnificent Two Trees. The elder, Telperion, is silvery; Laurelin, the younger, is golden. A flower from Telperion created the moon, and Telperion's sap created the second-making of the brightest stars. A fruit from Laurelin created the sun. As you come back to where you are, thank Varda for everything, and remember your experiences.

Keep a Journal

It is vital to keep a journal so that you can record your impressions, journeys, research, findings, symbols, messages, and anything else that enriches your relationship with the Star Queen. Besides, you need a place to practice drawing different stars! No matter in what form she appears to you, do your best to draw or paint it.

May your spiritual adventures with the Star Queen be uplifting, inspirational, healing, enlightening—even transformational—and most of all, fun! Mine are!

RESOURCES

Burk, Kevin. (2001). *Astrology: Understanding the Birth Chart*. St. Paul, MN: Llewellyn.

Robson, Vivian E. (1923, 2nd ed.1979). *The Fixed Stars and Constellations in Astrology*. York Beach, ME: Samuel Weiser.

Tolkien, J. R. R. (1954-55). *The Lord of the Rings*. London: Houghton-Mifflin.

Tolkien, Christopher (Editor). (1977). *The Silmarillion*. London: Houghton-Mifflin.

Internet Resources

Encyclopedia Mythica: www.pantheon.org

Free astrology lessons at www.astrologyforthesoul.com/cours.html.

Free astrology charts at www.astro.com.

Horary astrology at www.skyscript.co.uk/horary_intro.html.

Locations and mythologies of fixed stars at http://users.winshop
.com.au/annew; www.astrologycom.com/fixedstars.html.

Star symbols at www.meta-religion.com/Esoterism/Symbols/star_
symbols.htm.

Tië eldaliéva, "The Elven Path" at www.thehiddenrealm.org.

Calantirniel *has practiced many forms of natural spirituality since the early 1990s. She lives in western Montana with her husband and teenage daughter, while her older son is in college. She is a professional astrologer, tarot card reader, and dowser; and she became a certified master herbalist in 2007. She has an organic garden, crochets professionally, and is co-creating Tië eldaliéva, meaning the Elven Spiritual Path. Find out more by visiting http://www.myspace.com/aartiana.*

Illustrations: Carolyn Vibbert

The Fabulous Magical Frog

Michelle Skye

I admit it. I love their soft skin and their little pop-eyes, their long tongues, and powerful hind legs. My house is decorated with frog statues and mini frog figurines. Frog pictures adorn the walls and frog necklaces rest in my jewelry box. Why this obsession with a small amphibious creature that would prefer mud and muck to the wood flooring in my living room? I can't rightly say, but I can trace my first recognition of this love to a sixth grade biology lesson.

Sixth grade is that odd time in every preteen's life when things just don't fit. You're not a teenager, but you're also

not a child. You're neither part of the elementary school nor the high school. You can go about in the world on your own, but you must rely on others to get to specific places. You can walk but not drive, go to the movies but not on a date. You are stuck in a time of transition, valiantly floundering about in an effort to find a place, a personality, an identity that fits. It's not easy!

And frog understands this dilemma on an intimate level, for frog spends its entire life stuck between water and earth, needing both to survive. As a creature of water and earth, frog connects humanity to the idea of transitions, of a deep, intuitive change within. When frog hops into your life, she brings with her profound transformations that will affect your worldview, your sense of self, and your deep-seated beliefs. Small but powerful, frog heralds inner growth that radiates out to encompass all, cosmically shifting the world, ever so slightly.

Living within the swamps, the primordial ooze, the sticky water and muddy earth, frog is inherently connected to the Goddess. Therefore it is not surprising that Heket (Heqet), the most popular and well-known frog deity, is a woman or, to be more specific, a woman with a frog head. A lesser-known Egyptian goddess, Heket, was immensely popular throughout ancient Egypt due to her association with pregnancy and childbirth. Pregnant mothers would wear frog amulets to protect their unborn children and ensure healthy births. Heket was seen as especially helpful during the later stages of labor (truly a magical, transitional time!). Mother of fertility, childbirth, and grain germination, Heket was the force behind the bringing forth of life. As her husband Khnum shaped each human being's body on his potter's wheel, so Heket breathed the life force into the clay before depositing it into the welcoming embrace of the watery womb, a place swamp-like in its heat, shifting land mass, and watery edges.

The fecundity of the frog, as embodied in the goddess Heket, takes root in many other cultures as well. In several Native American cultures, the frog is the symbol of quiet, contemplative fertility, often associated with birth and female reproduction. Frog (along with the snake and the salamander) is depicted as the guardian of fresh-water lakes and ponds. Indeed, if a drought occurs, several native legends point to the frog as the originator of the problem. She is shown as having woven a dam or basket that holds back the waters. Another plot twist describes the frog guardian as having swallowed up all the water, housing it in her belly. In order to free the water, the hero must either destroy the dam, or punch or stab the frog's bloated stomach. The released waters are filled with all manner of water plants and animals which, in turn, provide nourishment for the hungry and thirsty humans. Frog, in this case, holds the waters until the growth is complete, much as a mother holds the unborn child in her womb until her waters are released.

Frog's association with water extends beyond lakes and streams and womb-water to the life-giving rain which falls from the sky. In Navaho tradition, frog has power over rain and sends it whenever he is asked by humans. Half way across the globe, in India, "frog marriages" are performed to alleviate droughts and bring about rain. Villagers gather a pair of male and female frogs from a nearby pond and decorate them with vermilion-colored kumkum, a substance made from haldi, turmeric, and alum traditionally used to create a bindi or dot on the forehead. With the chanting of Vedic hymns and the tying of the *moodu mullu* (three knots), the frogs are declared married and released back into the pond, with prayers to the goddess Muthyalamma for rain. A similar rain ritual involves gathering a pair of frogs, decorating them with vermilion kumkum and wrapping them in a piece of cloth. The frogs are then carried through the streets in an informal procession, amid dancing, drumming, and horn blowing. Once the procession is finished, the frogs are placed back in the water. This frog parade is repeated for three days in a row and is done to appease the deity Muthyalamma, who is thought to prevent disease and answer all prayers.

In these Hindu rituals, frog serves as the messenger between the people and the Goddess. Once again, she is seen as not being entirely of one world, but, rather, comfortable in two. Earth and water, physical and spiritual, life and death and rebirth, frog transcends her physical space to soar beyond her limitations. She is a link to the divine, yet a grounded force that listens and helps her human brethren. However, frog's intellect and wit are often overlooked due to her small size, as shown in the Angolan tale "How Frog Went to Heaven."

In this story, frog serves as a messenger between a human man and the Sky Maiden. He travels up to heaven several times, by hiding in the Sky Maiden's water jug, in order to bring letters and messages and gifts back and forth between the Sky Maiden in heaven and the young man on earth. At this point in the story, he is the granter of wishes as he seeks to fulfill the desire of the young man.

Frog can be tricky and, with the slippery nature of his skin, can slide just out of our reach. In the Angolan tale, frog eventually lures the Sky Maiden down to earth. However, just as he is about to lead the Sky Maiden to the young man, he tells her the truth of his actions. Impressed by the resourcefulness of the frog, the Sky Maiden decides to marry him instead of the young man. She takes the frog back to heaven with her, where they continue to live today.

Frog has an uncanny ability to achieve nearly impossible feats, through intelligence, persistence, and an ability to think outside of the box. In the Angolan myth, he travels to heaven and wins an immortal bride. In a tale from the Kootenai Indian nation (in California), frog confounds a faster animal and wins a race. In a story similar to "The Tortoise and the Hare," the speedy and egotistical antelope challenges the small and humble frog to a race. Frog accepts and beats the antelope at his own game. When the antelope asks the frog how he won the race, the frog admits that he hid his relatives along the race route. After each hop, the frog would hide in the long grass by the edge of the race route. Once hidden, a new (and fully refreshed) frog would continue the race. Because of his large family, each frog had only to hop once, thus never tiring and allowing the frog(s) to win. Frog's cooperation and lack of personal ego propels

him forward to win the race. His ability to change and adapt allows him to see and try new ways of tackling a difficult situation.

In the medieval era, frog's adaptability linked her to transmutation, alchemy, and magic. Borrowing from classical Greek and Roman writers who gifted frogs with wondrous, supernatural powers, the members of the Inquisition often linked frogs (and toads) to witches, using them as evidence of sorcery. In numerous sixteenth-century engravings, frogs are displayed as witches' familiars, animals that the inquisitors believed were inhabited by demons and worked with the witch. *The Malleus Maleficarum*, or *Witches' Hammer*, labels frogs as one of the "impure" animals because of the medieval belief that frogs could be created through putrefaction, the infusion of a small element of live matter into rotten or putrefying flesh. The putrefaction process serves as a symbol of frog's innate ability to transmute the mud, the rotten experiences of our past, into new life. As the ultimate example of rebirth, it shows that, even during the deadly era of the Inquisition, frog's fertile, transformative nature could not be nullified.

The Witches' Hammer often associates frogs with the turning of men into beasts, altering frog's transformative power to suit their own religious needs. The book goes on further to explain that witches would go into ponds to gather frog semen for the putrefaction creation process, once again bringing the essence of the frog full-circle, back to the watery, fertile, rebirthing nature of the earliest frog symbolism in world mythology.

Frog Magic

Frog can bring her adaptability, her fertility, her quiet power and hidden knowledge to work wonders in our lives. During times of indecision, frog can help you see things from a new perspective, clearing away the muck of confusion, in order to truly view the separation between earth and water. When you are in need of new ideas or new beginnings, frog brings her cyclic nature into your life, allowing you to let go of the past and press forward into the future. Birth, death, and rebirth are her calling card and she is comfortable in the transitory time between each station of being.

If you are birthing a baby, an artistic project, or a new career, frog can assist in containing your creativity until you are ready to allow it to flow forth over the land, creating fertile soil for your inspiration to take root. Frog's gentle nature gives you the freedom to pursue your dreams and the confidence and courage to manifest them in the everyday. The magic of frog is, at once, intensely personal and profoundly universal. Her lessons and knowledge touch upon the sacred. They are transitional and transformative.

This is frog's power. Working with her, you are changed on the deepest level, shifting your relationship with yourself, with others in your community, and with the world around you. She is the regenerator, the soother, the kind companion, the trickster, the transformer, the creator. She is the Goddess incarnate.

Connecting with Frog

Items needed: a large blue or green bowl, a small frog pendant or statue, chamomile incense, a lighter or book of matches, dried blue lotus herb, fly agaric (*Amanita muscaria*) mushroom caps, and sacred water (optional).

NOTE: *Amanita muscaria* has been linked to numerous shamanic, visionary traditions around the world. However, it is listed as poisonous by the FDA. Do not ingest *Amanita muscaria*, under any circumstances. If you are uncomfortable with fly agaric, use a common, edible mushroom instead.

Fill your bowl with water, the purer, the better. If you have water from a sacred and holy place (such as the Chalice Well in England or the Ganges River), add three drops to the bowl. Set it down in a comfortable location, making sure all the other items are within easy reach. Light your chamomile incense and concentrate on its purification qualities. Wave the incense over the bowl and the water, requesting that it cleanse and purify the items. Do the same thing for the frog pendant or statue. When the items are sufficiently cleansed, hold the incense over the water and say:

Chamomile, as an herb of purification and abundance, you are forever linked to frog and her energy. I ask you to aid her entrance into my life.

Place the incense down near the bowl of water, making sure that the smoke wafts over the water for the rest of the ceremony.

Next, gather the lotus blossoms in your hands. Hold them above the bowl and say:

Blue lotus, as an herb of creation and rebirth,
you are forever linked to frog and her energy.
I ask you to aid her entrance into my life.

Sprinkle the blue lotus flowers in your water, thinking of their connection to rebirth, transformation, and rejuvenation. Take three small mushroom caps and remove their stems, if necessary. Hold them over the water and say:

Fly agaric, as an herb of fertility and alteration,
you are forever linked to frog and her energy.
I ask you to aid her entrance into my life.

Drop the mushroom caps into the bowl, considering their connection to change, mystery, and the divine.

Finally, hold the frog pendant or statue in your hands, over the bowl of water. Sense the wonder and quiet power of frog and state aloud your intention to access it. Give at least three reasons why you wish to become more familiar with frog's essence. State them out loud, over the bowl, allowing your breath to mingle with the water, the incense, and the herbs. When you are done, drop the pendant or statue in the bowl. Watch as it sinks to the bottom. The moment it hits the bottom, anoint yourself with the water, behind your ears and at your temples, wrists, and third eye (forehead). For the next three days, anoint yourself in the morning and the evening (preferably at the transition times of dawn and dusk) in the same manner. On the fourth day, remove the mushroom caps and lotus flowers and dispose of them in a sacred manner. (If you choose to use *Amanita muscaria*, make sure no animals will be able to find them and eat them. You wouldn't want a household pet to get poisoned!) Take out the frog pendant or statue and either put it on or place it in your pocket. While carrying the frog emblem, pour the water onto the ground outside. You can now access the power of frog at any time!

Michelle Skye *has been a practicing eclectic witch for over thirteen years and has been working with the fey since she was a child. Although solitary, she is active in the pagan community. Michelle presents workshops and classes in southeastern Massachusetts at local stores and at Pagan Pride Days, as well as at Womongathering, a goddess festival in Pennsylvania. Michelle is a published author in both the mundane and magical communities. Her new book* Goddess Alive!, *published by Llewellyn, is available in bookstores now. Look for the next book in the goddess series,* Goddess Afoot, *in 2008. Michelle's interests include (but are not limited to) the feminine divine, goddess magick, nature divination, tree legend and lore, yoga, Middle Eastern dance, faeries, elemental magic, and mythology. You can contact Michelle through her Web site: www.MichelleSkye.com.*

Illustrations: Neil Brigham

Taking Their Leave

Deborah Blake

Whether you call a group a coven, a circle, or a grove, witches who practice in a group know that the ties formed by practicing magick together on a regular basis can be as strong as or stronger than any of the other bonds in our lives. Our covens are the families we choose and sometimes our relationships with the people within our group are as deep and as lasting as those we have with the families into which we were born.

Like the rest of our existence, our covens are subject to change and transformation; very few groups that last for longer than a year or two will end up looking or acting the same as they did when they were first formed. This is not a bad thing, in general. After all, there can be no growth without change, and the composition and function of our groups should reflect the cycle of growth and renewal that witches follow in all aspects of their lives.

Oftentimes over the course of the years, coven members will come and go: people drift away or lose interest, decide the group is not right for them, or simply don't "fit." There are times, however, when a group member departs that both the coven and the departing member need to find a way to cope with the impending separation. Whether the loss is permanent, as in a move away or even a death, or temporary, as when a member leaves town for an extended period of time, this separation can be a difficult adjustment to make.

This happened recently to my group, Blue Moon Circle. One of our circle-sisters, a longtime group member, took a job in Vietnam that would require her to be gone for two years. It was an exciting opportunity and we were happy for her, but at the same time we mourned the loss of her presence in our circle and in our lives. Neither she nor we could be certain that she would find her way back to us again.

As high priestess, it was my responsibility to find some way to ease this transition for everyone involved, and to help us all to make our peace with the changes to come. My goal was to come up with a ritual through which we could create a permanent link to Zanna, the circle member who was leaving; one which would bind her closely enough that she felt that she was still a part of the group even while she was far away, yet loosely enough that if she someday wished to undo the bond between us, she could do so without difficulty.

As it turned out, Blue Moon Circle did this magickal work as two rituals, one on the new moon and one on the following full moon, but your group could easily combine the two if that would work better for those involved.

Creating a Group Staff

We had talked for some time about creating a staff for the group, one that could be used by any member to cast the circle, and which would replace our current speaking stick, which was simply an appealing piece of "found" wood about a foot long. I decided that this would be the perfect time to do this project, while Zanna was still around to add her energy to the staff. The group's existing speaking stick, on the other hand, would be decorated by everyone else in the group at the same time we made the staff, so that Zanna could take it with her on her travels (thus taking some of Blue Moon Circle's energy with her).

To do this project, you will need the following items, or whatever substitutions feel right to your group:

A tall piece of wood to use as a staff—it should be about as tall as your tallest member, or whatever size feels comfortable to you. Found wood is best, if you have trees in the area that you can scavenge amongst. Any kind of wood is fine, as long as it is dry, sturdy, and reasonably smooth, although a few kinds of trees are particularly appropriate for use as witches' staffs; apple, oak, or maple are especially powerful. If you can't find a suitable piece, it is fine to buy a plain staff. The point here is that you are making this staff together and combining your energies and imaginations to create a beautiful and useful tool for your group—the origins of the wood are not that important.

A shorter piece of wood about a foot long. A wand works well, if you happen to have one. Again, it should be smooth and sturdy.

Tools for carving or wood-burning, and/or colored permanent markers. We used both a wood-burning tool and markers, and they

made for a nice combination of colorful and subtle. Be careful if using a wood-burner—they get hot! (If you're doing this outside, you also will need a place to plug it in, and a long extension cord.) It is a good idea to have a heat-resistant plate to rest the burner on, if using one.

- A long strip of leather, and some silver wire (the wire is helpful, but not necessary).

- A clear quartz crystal.

- Various small additional items, such as feathers, shells, and stones—each coven member should bring something to add that has special meaning to them.

- Glue, sealing wax, additional strips of leather or other means of attaching bits and pieces to the staff.

Once you've assembled all the components, gather together and cast a circle. Strictly speaking, this part of the ritual doesn't have to take place inside of the circle, but I think that it helps everyone to focus on the sacred nature of the project, and it also serves to contain the energy that you are directing into the staff.

Pass the staff around the circle and have each coven member take a turn adding his or her personal touches: writing a name (mundane or magickal), drawing symbols such as suns, moons, pentacles, or runes, and attaching the small objects that they are contributing. At the same time, someone else can be taking a turn decorating the smaller piece of wood that will be gifted to the departing coven member.

Once everyone has had a turn, the high priestess or high priest of the group can attach the crystal to the top of the staff. It is helpful to hollow out a space for it to fit into, and wetting the leather before wrapping it around the crystal will help it to tighten up once it dries. For extra security and a magickal boost, you can wrap a bit of silver wire around the crystal, too.

The finished staff and wand can be blessed and consecrated, and the wand given to the person who is leaving. Although this moment can be bittersweet, remember to have fun and enjoy working together—all that great energy of reverence and mirth will go into the tools and help you with your magickal work whenever you use them!

Ritual: The Ribbon Ceremony

This is essentially a continuation of the work you did in creating a group staff, and you can easily do them both together if you so desire. The ribbons we use for this part of the ritual symbolize the ties that bind your group together. I chose ribbons rather than something "tougher" like leather because the goal was to hold on loosely, not tightly. And, of course, they are beautiful and easy to write on; as witches, we often need to be creative and practical at the same time!

For this part of the ritual, you will need two lengths of ribbon, ¾-inch to one-inch wide. One should be about three feet long (at least six inches for every member of the group) and the other can be shorter, about two feet long. They can be any color, as long as they are light enough to use a pen on and have it be legible. Blue Moon Circle used pink for love and yellow for loyalty. You could also just use a plain cream or white to represent the Goddess. You'll also need permanent markers in various colors (it helps to have something to lean on while you're writing, especially if you are outside—we used the group Book of Shadows, but any flat portable surface will do).

Quiet background music, a sage smudge stick if you use one, and cakes and ales are nice for this ritual. This is a good occasion to have a real cake, and something special in the chalice—after all, you are celebrating each other, and what better basis for celebration could there be?

If you did the first part of this ritual separately, start now by casting your circle. This is the perfect time to bring out your newly created group staff. The high priest or high priestess can carry it around the outside of the circle to enclose your group in sacred space.

Pass the smudge stick around the circle and take extra care to cleanse yourselves of any negativity that you might have brought in with you from your mundane lives. For this part of the ritual you want to be able to focus clearly on your heart and spirit, and that's a lot easier to do if you're not worrying about the fight you had with your boss or whether or not your cat is eating the houseplants.

Call the quarters and invoke the Goddess (or both God and Goddess) as you usually do. Then sit down and make yourselves comfortable. As you did with the staff, you will pass the longer ribbon and some colored pens around your circle. Have each coven member take a turn writing down what they like and admire about the person who is leaving. For example, on Zanna's ribbon, people wrote that they admired her adventurous spirit, her loving heart, her courage, and so on.

While that is happening, the departing circle member takes the shorter ribbon and writes down everything about the group that he or she likes and will miss. Zanna wrote specific comments for each member of the group. As an example, this is what she wrote to me: "The space you hold for the sacred Goddess has changed me. Blessed be." She also added various symbols, the name of the group, and so on. Everything she wrote touched us deeply, and gave us a little piece of her to keep in our hearts.

Once everyone is finished, share what you have written with each other. Needless to say, when your coven reads these comments aloud, there will be laughter and probably a few tears. Take a few moments to feel the powerful energy of love, openness, and appreciation that you have brought to life in your circle. Then take that energy and put it into the spell by reading it out loud in unison to the coven member who is leaving. Visualize that person surrounded by the bright light of your group's love and energy, traveling safely no matter how far from you he or she goes. And expect a few more tears.

Spell for Saying Goodbye

We walked the sacred road as one
Brought together by fate and stars
Although our paths must part for now
In our hearts you're always ours
The circle stretches further now
The bond is bent but never broken
Our spirit still walks the way with you
Our love in all the words unspoken
Take our prayers and take our blessings
Journey safe and journey well
Know our thoughts will travel with you
And love will go to where you dwell
God and Goddess hold you safe
And if they choose to grant our boon
Someday we will meet again
And dance beneath the witches' moon

When you have finished, tie the shorter ribbon (the one written by the person leaving) around the group staff. This will serve
to bind his or her energy into the group energy. The longer ribbon,
with the comments written by the group, can be presented to the
departing coven member in a special box or pouch, along with any
small tokens you may want to pass on at the same time. That ribbon
will enable the group's energy to travel with the person who is leaving, no matter where he or she goes. In times of stress or difficulty,
the ribbon can be taken out and read, and it will be as if the coven is
right there, holding that person in a warm embrace.

Share your cakes and ale, and spend some time just enjoying each
other's company. When you are ready to open the circle, be sure to
thank the gods for bringing you together in the first place. Remember

that the wheel will turn around again, and that nothing is ever truly lost to us, but will someday spiral back along the great road we walk together.

If one of your coven members is dying, this ritual can be done exactly as written. If, however, your group has lost a member unexpectedly (as happened recently to the circle I started with), you can alter the ritual by either leaving out the wand and ribbon that would have been given to a departing member, or you can have one covener "stand in" for the person you have lost. You could also make the wand and ribbon for your covener and burn them afterward. The spell can be used just as it is written. May it give you peace.

Deborah Blake *is a Wiccan high priestess who has been leading her current group, Blue Moon Circle, for four years. She is the author of* Circle, Coven & Grove: A Year of Magickal Practice *(Llewellyn, 2007). Her second book,* Everyday Witch A to Z: An Amusing, Inspiring & Informative Guide to the Wonderful World of Witchcraft, *will be coming out in September 2008. Deborah was also a finalist in the Pagan Fiction Award Contest and her short story, "Dead and (Mostly) Gone" can be found in the* Pagan Fiction Anthology. *When not writing, Deborah runs The Artisans' Guild, a cooperative shop she founded with a friend. She is also a jewelry maker, tarot reader, an ordained minister, and an intuitive energy healer. She lives in a 100-year-old farmhouse in rural upstate New York with five cats who supervise all her activities, both magickal and mundane.*

Ilustrations: Kyle Fite

Seed Work

Trynen

If we don't change, we don't grow. If we don't grow, we aren't really living.
GAIL SHEEHY

Change and growth. Two simple words that seem to go hand in hand. Two simple words that most of us who walk a pagan path seem to reference often when speaking of our beliefs to others. Two simple words that often lie at the core of our spiritual practices, of our ideals and goals, of our studies, of our rites and workings. These words are found in many of our chants and songs, many of our rituals and prayers, and just about every book on the subject of Wicca and paganism authored over the last two or three dozen years.

Change and growth. Growth and change. They are for many the very foundations of the spiritual journey that is paganism. Through change we grow, through growth we journey further along our path . . . closer to our goals . . . closer to "balance" . . . to "oneness" . . . to a deeper, stronger connection with the Goddess and God.

Yet many of us find ourselves feeling as if we are at a standstill in this journey. The busy-ness of our day-to-day lives overtakes us, leaving us feeling disconnected and distant from our spiritual paths, distant from our goals, our hopes, and our dreams. Perhaps we have a strong desire to bring about change, but we're just not quite sure how to get there. Something seems to be lacking; we just aren't sure what this "something" is, let alone how to go about changing it. There's so much we want out of life, and we feel the urge to grow to our full potential—but how? Perhaps by taking a hint from nature itself.

All of nature is "growth" and "change." This is a very simple truth. Nature does not struggle to grow; it works with what it is presented, transforming and moving as necessary to produce results. If you build a fence too close to an oak tree, the tree will grow around that fence. In nature, life always moves on. So why isn't that the case with us? Why do we allow the obstacles we face, the roadblocks we experience along our paths, to bring us to a standstill? Why is it that we do not embrace growth and change? Why do we allow ourselves to be distant from nature's cycle of growth?

The Wheel of the Year

Growth and change are there for the taking. Their story is the story of the natural cycle of life, the story of the wheel of the year. This story weaves its way throughout our rites and rituals, throughout our workings and spells. It is a blessing! The blessing of a powerful story of growth and change, yet we often overlook it. We pass through the seasons, through the sabbats and esbats, without even realizing the wonderful opportunities we let slip away. The opportunities to find a deeper, stronger connection with nature, with the Goddess and God, and with ourselves. The opportunity to learn, to grow, to change, and to create the life we dream of living.

Opportunity is there for the taking. All you have to do is allow yourself to feel it. Allow yourself to become one with the cycle of growth and change through your rites, rituals, and celebrations. Plant the seed of that which you wish to grow in your life, and watch it blossom and grow to become a bountiful harvest!

THE COLD MOON

Our seed journey begins with the calm and quiet of January's Cold Moon. Just as the icy chill of winter leads us to the warmth and comfort of home, the long dark of deep winter nights lead us on a journey inward. This is a time for contemplation and asking oneself the tough questions, such as: What do I need to know for my life now? What are my goals, hopes, and dreams? What brought me here? What is it that I hope to achieve by walking this path? What changes must I make to promote growth in my life and to bring me closer to my goals?

The Cold Moon is the clean slate—the blank canvas—and the possibilities are endless! The brush is in your hands, the paints lay before you. What is it you will create? What do you wish to create?

There are many questions to ask yourself. Make this a part of your Cold Moon esbat. Take time to divine your own future. Use tarot, runes, the stillness of a cauldron full of water, the flickering flames of a ritual fire, or whatever means of divination you are most comfortable with.

Turn inward, meditate, seek guidance from the Goddess and God. Seek guidance as you ask yourself the toughest question of them all: What "seed" must I plant to ensure a bountiful harvest for my self?

IMBOLC AND THE QUICKENING MOON

Weeks pass. The darkness slowly gives way to light and Imbolc sabbat arrives. Imbolc is a time of purification. It is a time of blessing and preparation. Perhaps without even realizing it, you've set energy into motion by simply choosing to begin this journey. You've begun to gather the necessary tools, and have already devoted time and energy toward planning for a future harvest. Perhaps you've already chosen which "seed" you will plant, or perhaps not. It may take several more weeks before that knowledge comes to you with absolute certainty, and yet you do know that you will plant something. Energy is in motion! It gathers around you in anticipation, waiting for a direction in which to travel.

This is a time to prepare yourself for the work ahead. This is a time to wash yourself clean in the cauldron waters of rebirth. It is a time to cleanse and purify yourself, and to ask for the blessings of the Goddess and God to be upon your work . . . upon your journey . . . upon your seed.

As the Quickening Moon shines upon you, the energies of your seed grow stronger. They swirl around you, gaining speed and strength as your focus becomes even clearer. Celebrate this moment! Sing! Dance! Drum! Laugh! Feed the energy of change and nurture the energy of growth! Allow yourself to feel the joyousness of anticipation . . . anticipation of that which you *will* harvest! Know that it *is* going to manifest! Feel that it is going to manifest! Allow yourself to feel the joy of that realization—and celebrate it! This is the power of the Quickening Moon!

OSTARA AND THE STORM MOON

Our path brings us to the top of a hill. We stand and look out across a great, empty field. With a bag of possibilities we set out down the hill, ready to begin our work. The time of planting is upon us!

In our tradition, the Veryus tradition of Wicca, "The Planting of the Seed" is one of our most sacred ceremonies. Each member is given a slip of paper upon which they write the word, words, or statement that they feel best describes their Seed—that which they wish to grow in their life. Each person then rolls their slip of paper into a spiral and places it into the cauldron that rests at the center of the circle. The paper is lit and sacred flame transforms the Seed into energy within the womb of the great Mother Goddess.

When all Seeds have been planted within the cauldron, our high priestess pours a small amount of consecrated water—symbolic of the cauldron waters of rebirth—upon the ashes. The Seeds blend to become one Seed. Our high priestess then forms a womb within the soil of a potted flower . . . and holds this flower while our high priest pours this seed-water into that womb, and covers the Seed. The flower is then passed from covener to covener so that each might pour blessings upon the Seed. Then, the entire plant is placed within the cauldron, returning to the womb of the Great Mother to be born.

It is done. The Seed has been planted!

It is as simple as that. Yet it is a truly difficult thing to sit within the sacred circle with pen in hand and a blank slip of paper before you. You have to be completely honest with yourself as you state "This is my Seed." It is far tougher than it sounds! Choosing the Seed that is right and proper for you. Choosing the Seed that will serve as sort of an umbrella, covering all of that which you wish to change and to grow within your life. Choosing the Seed that is going to nourish you and carry you further along your path. Choosing that seed with absolute certainty.

Yet pen touches paper . . . words emerge . . . and somehow you just know that they are right. You feel it in your bones. And when you plant that Seed, you feel a moment of release, of excitement, like no other! It is a truly powerful and beautiful moment!

Our celebrations do not stop at the planting. They continue as we sing, dance, drum, chant, and weave energy around the cauldron to feed the energy of our Seed! Sending well-wishes of growth, strength, and fruitfulness with the knowledge that we *will* have a bountiful harvest!

Yet we must remember that with any planting, there must also be destruction. Before a Seed may be planted, soil must be disturbed because there must be a disruption if growth is to occur. This is the energy of the Storm Moon. By planting your Seed you have set a powerful energy of change and growth into motion. Change and growth will occur. The Cold Moon may have been the calm before the storm . . . and the Storm Moon is that storm. Powerful changes are now in effect and nothing will ever be the same! Celebrate the beauty and power of change! Feel the energy and excitement in the air as the wind picks up and the lightning strikes!

The Wind Moon

Deep within the womb of the Great Mother, our Seed rests. The warmth of the sun calls it to life and the first stirrings occur. Energy moves within and the first tiny shoot pushes its way through moist soil, to break the surface. Two tiny leaves burst open—arms stretching to greet the sun—and the breath of life enters our seedling!

The Wind Moon is that breath of life. It fills us, lifts us, carries us higher. It nourishes, shapes, and forms us. For it is also the wind of change. We breathe deeply, for this air is fresh and pure. We see those first visible signs of growth—that tiny seedling pushing through the soil—and we feel a certain sense of rebirth and renewal. We cannot help but feel excited as we anticipate the wonderful things which lie ahead. We are being called to life. We are being called to change and to grow. The winds lift us high like a kite rising into the clouds. This new, fresh life feels so strong that we cannot help but be moved by it. Celebrate the beauty of this moment. Invite the powers of air into your life! Fill yourself with its nourishment. Breathe deeply and know that the winds of change are blowing strong within your life.

BELTANE AND THE FLOWER MOON

Though spring arrived over a month and a half ago, for many, spring's call doesn't feel strong until Beltane. The sun grows warmer with each passing day, and the air is filled with the scent of new leaves and fragrant flowers. One cannot help but feel alive!

As the Goddess and God come closer together, the effects of the growing sun upon the earth become more and more apparent. You see it in everything from the behavior of animals to the blossoming of flowers to the activity of people who have been hibernating within for far too long. Beltane calls us to life and to celebration of the blessings of life.

The Flower Moon is just that—the time of flowering, of blossoming. We look upon our Seed plants and see those first tiny flowers—the promise of future fruits—and we smile. We know that change is in effect. We know that we are growing. Perhaps we've already begun to see hints of our future harvest through little successes and transformations. We dance under the Flower Moon in celebration of the beauty and blessings of the Goddess and God and of the beauty and blessings of nature—of life!

LITHA AND THE STRONG SUN MOON

The sun grows stronger with each passing day. As summer approaches, our Seed plant experiences an enormous growth spurt! The once tiny stalk with a few small leaves and flowers is now a strong stem with full leaves and perhaps even the first hints of fruit. It grows taller and taller each day, reaching toward the sun—rising to life!

With each new leaf and each new fruit, we feel the growth within our lives. We begin to realize that magic truly is at work and nothing is the same. On Litha, we look around us and see the fullness and beauty of nature and know that we are a part of it. We celebrate the beauty and magic—of all that is—and dance the dance of life among the flicker of fireflies on a warm summer night. Change is in effect—we can feel it!

We must take care, though, for our work is far from over! Just as the sun has called our Seed to life . . . so can it take that life away. Though we celebrate the milestones we reach along the way, we cannot allow ourselves to fall into the trap of believing that our harvest is a done deal. There is still a great deal of work to be done to protect what we have already achieved. The sun gives life to the Seed—calls it to awaken and to grow—yet the sun can also dry the soil, scorch the plant, and leave a wilted and withered shadow of what could have been. And as if threat of drought isn't enough, we have pests to deal with, ranging from hungry caterpillars eyeing the leaves to neighbors keeping an eye on that rather large fruit that is ripening and hoping to get their hands on it before we do. We must protect our Seed plant and keep our work nourished. This is the lesson of the Strong Sun Moon. Celebrate what you've achieved, but don't stop now. Keep working the field . . . keep a watchful eye over the crop . . . nourish and protect what you've brought to life! Seek guidance and strength that you might continue to do what must be done to ensure the ripening of the fruit.

The Blessing Moon

The sun grows stronger still. The long days of summer bring us a Seed plant heavy with fruit and blessing. Perhaps it's so full that it can no longer support it's own weight! This is the time we must step in to support our plant with stakes and twine—reaffirming our commitment to see things through to the end.

The Blessing Moon shines upon us and we know that the harvest is just around the bend. Perhaps we've already been able to enjoy a wonderful taste of the blessings that lie in store for us. We feel the change in our lives. We're not quite sure how it has happened, we just know that it has.

We stand on the edge of our little field, leaning upon our garden rake for a brief rest after a day spent weeding and caring for our crop. We wipe the sweat from our brow, look over what we have achieved, and smile like we've never smiled before.

Look at what you have and at what you have achieved. How is life different than it was four months ago at Ostara? How is it different than it was seven months ago at the Cold Moon? How far have you come since last year's Blessing Moon?

See the blessings that are in your life. See your spiritual path, your family and friends . . . your home . . . your food . . . your clothing . . . your career . . . your education . . . your talents . . . your hopes . . . your dreams. See and feel all that you have been blessed with, and take a moment to to celebrate it! Know that more blessings are just around the corner, waiting for you to accept them into your life, and enjoy the nourishment they offer you.

Lughnassadh and the Corn Moon

The wind blows and fields of golden grain move in shimmering waves beneath the sun. Crows call from a field of corn, where they weave amongst the stalks, hoping for a meal as full ears ripen and corn silk sways. Deep green leaves turn golden, as mature plants slouch under the weight of dozens of heavy, ripening tomatoes that seem as if they're about to burst as they await picking.

It is time!

The journey that brought you to this point has been long; it has been tough at times, and smooth at others. Some days you enjoyed a clear path and a beautiful view. Other days you encountered a rocky path, covered in weeds, blocked by thorns, and surrounded by forest so thick you couldn't see more than a few feet into the darkness. There have been days when you had to spend your time weeding, and days when you could lounge and enjoy the sun. And it has been worth it!

You reach out and take hold of the fruit before you and, with a gentle twist, pluck it from the vine. Closing your eyes, you bring it to your mouth and take a long anticipated bite. The harvest has begun! Through Lughnassadh and the Corn Moon we dance amongst our fields, tasting fruit from every plant, smiling and laughing, and enjoying every minute of our harvest. We honor the Goddess and God, and thank them for the blessings they've given to us. Happiness fills our hearts as we enjoy the fruits of our labors, and share our bountiful harvest with our family and friends!

Once again, we look at what we have—at what we have been able to achieve—and we smile. This is a time of celebration!

MABON AND THE HARVEST MOON

The harvest continues, and at the time of Mabon and the Harvest Moon we find ourselves surrounded by baskets overflowing with fruit. We know our hard work truly has paid off—it has been a bountiful harvest. Many changes in our lives over the six months since Ostara. We look behind us and see that we have come so far along our path and have had so much grow around us that we can no longer see that hill we stood on a mere six months ago. We have changed. We have grown.

This is a very deep realization. We've had time to spend with our harvest . . . time to sample each of the fruits from each of the plants and trees. We've had time to reflect, and time to contemplate.

We continue to gather, to fill our baskets, to enjoy our fruits. We continue to celebrate what we have achieved. Yet we also can't help but feel a bit of a loss. We cannot help but feel as if we've been over-looking something—something important.

We think back to what was and begin to realize that we have had to sacrifice a bit of ourselves in order to get to where we are today. We look out over our field and realize that there have been many sacrifices to bring us to this point. The earth has sacrificed a bit of herself to feed the plants. The plants have sacrificed a bit of them-selves to provide the fruit. The fruit has sacrificed itself to nourish and sustain us.

As we look upon our field, recognizing this moment, the wind picks up once more—a bit colder than you seem to remember it be-ing before. You realize that the sun is not as warm as it was a week ago. The sun has sacrificed itself to lend life to this cycle. It is wan-ing, and just as it once called all to life, it now whispers to all that it is time to rest.

We begin to gather the last of our fruits. We gather with family and friends to share in moments and feasts of gratitude. Our work slows, and we find ourselves with more and more time to think . . . to reflect . . . to contemplate. We're beginning to turn inward once more.

Samhain and the Blood Moon

The fields lie bare. What were once vibrant green vines now stand as twisted, dry, brown remnants. Winds blow gold and rust-colored leaves in spirals. Harvesting tools rest silently in sheds. The warmth of the sun seems to be but a memory.

There was a time when Samhain and the Blood Moon marked the days of preparing for the dark cold months of winter ahead.

The people would look over their livestock, choosing which animals would sustain them through the lean times and which animals would sustain to give birth to the new herd in spring. Meat would be cured, fruit and vegetables would be preserved and stored for use throughout the winter months.

And so it is with us. So it is with our own harvest.

We look over our harvest stock and see an abundance of fruit—more than we could ever hope to consume before the next harvest. What shall we do with it?

This is the lesson of the Blood Moon. It's time to choose. Don't let your harvest go to waste! Yes, take some to nourish you now, but be sure to preserve the rest so that it might continue to nourish you through the dark cold winter, and through all of your future days. Let this harvest provide the Seed for the next.

And as days pass and the Samhain sabbat arrives, we begin to turn deeper inward. We turn to the warmth of home and the love of friends and family. We think of those who have gone before . . . of the loved ones we have lost . . . of our ancestors. We seek their guidance, that we might learn what we must learn and continue to grow beyond the harvest.

The Mourning Moon

The autumn days of October turn into the pre-winter days of November. The winds carry a chill and perhaps the first frost can be seen in the early morning hours. Days grow short as the sun has passed, sacrificing itself to the harvest. The earth grows cold and silent.

Our thoughts grow long. We look back over our harvest, with time to examine what we might have missed amid the excitement of fresh fruits and new life. We see things that were hidden before. Deep thoughts emerge, and with them, deep questions.

Was my harvest as bountiful as it could have been? Was my fruit as sweet as it could be? Did I miss something? Was the Seed that I planted truly the Seed I needed to plant?

Perhaps doubts lead to disappointments. Perhaps, in looking back, you can't help but feel that you planted apples, yet what you truly wanted—truly needed—was peaches. Perhaps you feel as if your fruit was bitter, having never ripened the way you had hoped for. Perhaps you feel as if there simply wasn't enough. Perhaps, none of this is true; perhaps it all just seems too good to be true.

For some, the Mourning Moon brings about just that—mourning for opportunities missed, for fruit allowed to spoil, or simply for that which once was and had to be left behind for new life to flourish.

Yet for others, the Mourning Moon is a "gratitude moon." It is less about mourning a loss, and more about honoring a sacrifice. Whether it is the sun's sacrifice to feed a new cycle of growth or your own sacrifices to overcome your obstacles and promote growth and change in your life, this is a time of honoring that which has passed, to bring you to that which is now. This is a time to show gratitude, to gather in Thanksgiving for all that is, has been, or ever will be in your life.

YULE AND THE LONG NIGHTS MOON

Winter calls to us with icy whispers and the frosty embrace of the Long Nights Moon. Even amid the hustle and bustle of the holidays, there's a calm and quiet about this time that leads us inward. One cycle is ending and another waits to begin.

We look back over the calendar year and see how far we've come. It feels like yesterday that we chose our Seed, yet, it also feels as if that time was many years ago—perhaps thousands of miles ago, too. We've come far in our journey. We've changed. We've grown.

The sun rises on Yule morning . . . fresh . . . new . . . reborn. Though the coldest days of winter still remain to be seen, we know deep inside that from this point on, with each passing day, the sun grows in strength. With each passing day, we grow closer to that moment when the sun will call us to life once more.

We greet the newborn sun with great anticipation, for we recognize the new opportunities it brings! Looking at our stores of preserved harvest fruits, we smile, knowing that just around the bend there is a hill, and from that hill we'll see a vast empty field—a blank canvas, a clean slate.

Yes, we smile as we gaze at the Long Nights Moon . . . at the reborn sun. We smile and turn inward to the warmth of home. There's much thinking to do. The Cold Moon will be upon us soon and a new Seed must be chosen!

May all of your Seeds grow strong . . . May all of your harvests be bountiful and abundant . . . May all of your fruits be sweet . . . And may the blessings of growth and change be upon you!

Trynen *is a third-degree initiate of the Veryus Tradition, and he is honored to serve as high priest for the coven Sacred Flame. He describes himself as "artist-writer-thinker-human," and his path as "pagan with Wiccan tendencies." He lives in Connecticut with his best friend (who also happens to be his wife), their two young children, and one rather energetic ferret. He'd like to dedicate this piece to his family and to the members of Sacred Flame. Their love and friendship truly is the greatest blessing of them all.*

Illustrations: Rik Olson

Some Facts (and Fiction) About the Ouija Board

Eileen Troemel (Dragonlady)

The Ouija board is one technique for contacting spirits that has a reputation for being manipulated and used for evil purposes. I have delved into many types of divining, from numerology, tarot, and coin tossing, to pendulums, psychics, and palm reading. Like many people, I am fascinated with connecting to those who have passed, with receiving one more message from a loved one.

Laura, a good friend of mine, connects with spirits and she passes on messages from those spirits to folks they have left behind. Laura told me

that she uses the Ouija board in a non-traditional way. She uses a piece of jewelry, like a necklace or a ring, dangling from a string as a pendulum. I was a skeptic, but on more than one occasion I watched her hold the pendulum and get messages.

At first, I believed she was swinging the pendulum on her own, but I asked who was there for me. Using a pendulum made from my necklace, she got the initials of my father. My dad passed long before I met Laura so I didn't think she knew his name. I went through a list of questions, most of which Laura could not know the answers to, and I got answers to all of them.

At one point she stopped reading for me because she said my father was very angry. She dropped the necklace and walked away from the reading. While the topic under discussion was one that would have angered my dad, a small part of me was skeptical that she could become so overwhelmed with emotion. I thought perhaps she was just tired and needed a break.

Then, Laura challenged me to learn this skill. I tried on a few occasions at her house with her Ouija board. She handed me the pendulum (made from my ring), but it just dangled and did not move. I got no results at all.

Laura's Pendulum Method

Laura's Ouija board was passed down to her from her mother as a child, but she set it aside because the parents of her friends disapproved, thinking it was evil. Years later, Laura began exploring different ways of working with it again. She followed her instincts and put aside the planchette.

With her individualized pendulum, Laura instructs the seeker to focus on a single question, either out loud or in their head. Then she dangles the jewelry over the Ouija board and waits for an answer.

My sister, Teri, made her first attempt at divining this way at a gathering, but in a room full of noisy people, she was too easily distracted.

Teri and I were heading off to a three-day retreat when Laura suggested we take her Ouija board with us. I thought it would be a waste of suitcase space, but Laura had been such a wonderful person that I couldn't say no to her.

Teri and I drove through the hills of western Wisconsin, enjoying the beauty of the natural landscape and stopping at a natural spot we both connected to in our own way. Later in the evening, after relaxing and enjoying the beautiful scenery from our hotel balcony, we decided to clear off the coffee table and try working with the

Ouija board. I took out a pendulum, closed my eyes to focus while she asked question—and waited. Teri watched the board, because I find it is easier to focus when my eyes are closed. We had an informal circle, with our single candle lit in a Kwan Yin statue.

At first nothing happened. The pendulum hung straight down, not moving even the slightest bit. I thought to myself that I knew this would be a waste of time. I offered my sister a chance to try again, but she encouraged me to continue.

We asked if there was a spirit there to talk to us. The pendulum swung slightly toward no. We both laughed. Teri said, "Then who was moving the pendulum?" After that we began to ask more questions. We asked if our dad was there. My pendulum swung just a little toward "yes," as if in response to a gentle breeze.

... there seem to be two opinions when it comes to the Ouija board. One belief is that it is just a game and the movement of the planchette comes from the user's subconscious mind. The other belief is that this is a spiritual tool ...

We kept asking questions and receiving answers. At one point we both said we love and missed Dad, and I almost immediately burst into tears. The pendulum was swinging wildly to yes. We knew that he was sending his love back to us. I was overwhelmed with the fierce love I received from him and couldn't go on.

After a short break from the intense emotions, I continued to use the Ouija board to talk to Dad. We asked about our lives and his. We covered the whole family. We asked if there were others there and

got a resounding yes, yet the only one who spoke to us through the Ouija was Dad.

Sometimes the pendulum would swing wildly and other times it would just sway gently. I could almost feel my father's hand on top of mine pushing it toward one answer or another. My hand grew warm like it was enveloped in his. My arm didn't tire as I expected it to—perhaps because I was so focused on the conversation or perhaps because my dad was there supporting me.

I'm not sure how much time we spent using the board to talk to dad. It seemed like we were in a different place and time. Everything else seemed to fade for me except the connection I had with my sister and my dad. It was a magical time filled with power and love.

I was astounded to have such a positive result, and I owed Laura a huge apology for being skeptical about her skill and technique. Combining the pendulum with the Ouija board creates a unique tool to communicate with spirits. Laura has taught me well.

As with any new divination technique, I wanted to learn a bit more about the Ouija board. I knew there was a stigma attached, so I went into research mode.

Origin of the Ouija Board

I discovered a variety of beliefs. The current board and all the patents belong to Parker Brothers, who in the mid-1960s purchased it from the Fuld family. The Fuld family held these patents and had made the boards since the late 1800s, and the popularity of the board fluctuated with the spiritualist movement. It seems the board itself evolved from the practice of table tipping and automatic writing.

Some sources claim this divination technique dates back to ancient cultures, but there is much skepticism on this point. There is one reference to a pendulum dish, which was a round dish with letters on the outer rim, being used in Roman times. This is interesting to me since it so closely relates to how Laura instinctively changed. While some research indicates this technique

My personal experience taught me that even with my own skepticism I could do a divination technique I wasn't necessarily comfortable with.

may date back as far as the ancient Egyptians, it is not definitive and the sources are vague. Indisputable, though, are the modern patents. The earliest but lesser known patent is for a talking board in London, England, in 1854. The Ouija brand was patented in the U.S. in 1890.

The stigma of the Ouija board seems to have begun in 1972 with the movie *The Exorcist*. Prior to that, the board was used to communicate with dead relatives and other spirits. *The Exorcist* birthed a wave of movies that portrayed Ouija boards as tools for evil spirits to possess or cause harm to the user.

In general, there seems to be two opinions when it comes to the Ouija board. One belief is that it is just a game and the movement of the planchette comes from the user's subconscious mind. The other belief is that this is a spiritual tool, which may or may not bring in "evil" spirits, depending on how it is used.

My research revealed the following suggestions for using a board (numbers in parenthesis refer to resources listed at the end of this article):

- Place board between users so all have easy reach for the planchette (3, 8)

- Place fingers lightly on planchette (3)

- Invite a spirit to join and ask for a willing spirit in order to keep out the negative (3)

- Ask a question—only one at a time (3, 6, 8)

- Have a third person to act as a scribe or use a tape recorder so you can be clear on the messages coming through (7, 8)

- Always say goodbye and make sure the spirit does, so it doesn't linger after the session is done (7)

In addition to these basic steps, I found numerous suggestions on safety and care.

- Be serious and respectful (6, 8)

- Clean and keep the board free of dust with a soft, dry cloth (6)

- Use a slow circle around the board to get the planchette to move (8)

- Smudge the board with sage to purify and a white candle for protection (8)

- Use in a protective circle (7)

- Use a silver coin or wear silver jewelry to protect from harm (7)

- Say a prayer before using to keep away negative spirits (8)

- Use common sense with regard to the message you receive; if you are uncomfortable with the message, ask the messenger to leave (7, 8)

- Use at night (8)

- Use a wood board (7)

All of these are suggestions different sources offered to use the Ouija board. Some may work and some may not. Laura has done all her scrying during the day, and my successful attempt was at night. My personal experience taught me that even with my own skepticism I could do a divination technique I wasn't necessarily comfortable with. I just needed to focus on the technique and not concentrate on my skepticism. With practice and a belief in my abilities, I am able to connect to spirits using the Ouija board. I just needed to trust my own abilities.

RESOURCES (LIST ON PAGES 241–242)

1. http://zohrala.com/ouija/history.htm

2. http://www.mitchhorowitz.com/ouija.html

3. http://www.prairieghosts.com/ouija.html

4. http://www.damnedgames.com/cf_ouijahistory.html

5. http://stason.org/TULARC/education-books/ghost-stories/08-A lot-of-people-on-this-group-say-the-ouija-board-is-evi.html

6. http://zohrala.com/ouija/Howtouse.htm

7. http://stason.org/TULARC/education-books/ghost-stories/

   10-Are-there-any-rules-I-should-follow-when-using-the-Oui.html

8. http://www.damnedgames.com/cf_odirections.html

Additional Resources

http://www.museumoftalkingboards.com/ancient.html

http://www.cryptique.com/history.html

http://stason.org/TULARC/education-books/ghost-stories/07-What-is-a-ouija-board.html

http://stason.org/TULARC/education-books/ghost-stories/11-What-does-ouija-mean.html

http://stason.org/TULARC/education-books/ghost-stories/12-A-Brief-History-of-the-Ouija-Board.html

Eileen Troemel *resides in Milton, Wisconsin (near Madison). By day she is a clerical worker and at night she spends her spare time writing. Eileen was raised on a farm, and she continues to be inspired by the beauty and power in nature. Eileen's other interests include cooking, genealogy, reading, and crocheting.*

Illustrations: Carolyn Vibbert

The Lunar Calendar

March 2008 to March 2009

MARCH
```
S  M  T  W  T  F  S
                  1
2  3  4  5  6  7  8
9  10 11 12 13 14 15
16 17 18 19 20 21 22
23 24 25 26 27 28 29
30 31
```

APRIL
```
S  M  T  W  T  F  S
      1  2  3  4  5
6  7  8  9  10 11 12
13 14 15 16 17 18 19
20 21 22 23 24 25 26
27 28 29 30
```

MAY
```
S  M  T  W  T  F  S
            1  2  3
4  5  6  7  8  9  10
11 12 13 14 15 16 17
18 19 20 21 22 23 24
25 26 27 28 29 30 31
```

JUNE
```
S  M  T  W  T  F  S
1  2  3  4  5  6  7
8  9  10 11 12 13 14
15 16 17 18 19 20 21
22 23 24 25 26 27 28
29 30
```

JULY
```
S  M  T  W  T  F  S
      1  2  3  4  5
6  7  8  9  10 11 12
13 14 15 16 17 18 19
20 21 22 23 24 25 26
27 28 29 30 31
```

AUGUST
```
S  M  T  W  T  F  S
               1  2
3  4  5  6  7  8  9
10 11 12 13 14 15 16
17 18 19 20 21 22 23
24 25 26 27 28 29 30
31
```

SEPTEMBER
```
S  M  T  W  T  F  S
   1  2  3  4  5  6
7  8  9  10 11 12 13
14 15 16 17 18 19 20
21 22 23 24 25 26 27
28 29 30
```

OCTOBER
```
S  M  T  W  T  F  S
         1  2  3  4
5  6  7  8  9  10 11
12 13 14 15 16 17 18
19 20 21 22 23 24 25
26 27 28 29 30 31
```

NOVEMBER
```
S  M  T  W  T  F  S
                  1
2  3  4  5  6  7  8
9  10 11 12 13 14 15
16 17 18 19 20 21 22
23 24 25 26 27 28 29
30
```

DECEMBER
```
S  M  T  W  T  F  S
   1  2  3  4  5  6
7  8  9  10 11 12 13
14 15 16 17 18 19 20
21 22 23 24 25 26 27
28 29 30 31
```

2009

JANUARY
```
S  M  T  W  T  F  S
            1  2  3
4  5  6  7  8  9  10
11 12 13 14 15 16 17
18 19 20 21 22 23 24
25 26 27 28 29 30 31
```

FEBRUARY
```
S  M  T  W  T  F  S
1  2  3  4  5  6  7
8  9  10 11 12 13 14
15 16 17 18 19 20 21
22 23 24 25 26 27 28
```

MARCH
```
S  M  T  W  T  F  S
1  2  3  4  5  6  7
8  9  10 11 12 13 14
15 16 17 18 19 20 21
22 23 24 25 26 27 28
29 30 31
```

Journey for Water

You are in a canoe gently paddling in a calm and peaceful lake that is surrounded by a dense forest. You place the oar in your lap from time to time, letting the canoe slowly drift across the water. The water is gentle, lapping against the canoe. You notice a small cove up ahead and paddle toward it, taking in the warmth of the day. There is an osprey circling in flight overhead and a deer on the distant shoreline sipping water slowly from the lake, totally unaware of your presence. Entering the cove you see a small sandy beach in the center and a large boulder jutting out over the still water to the right. Standing on the boulder is a woman, wearing a white robe and a circlet around her head. She is looking toward you and smiling. You bring the canoe to the beach, where you leave it as you begin to walk to a narrow path that leads from the beach up to the boulder. You climb up onto the boulder and she opens her arms and embraces you completely. You feel the warmth and love of the Mother as she soothes every negative emotion that you have ever felt and places a kiss upon your brow. She removes all negative images from your memory, replacing them with love. You stand at the edge of the boulder and peer into the water below. With the Mother beside you, her protective arm around you, she shares the mystery of Water's healing energy. Then, she releases her embrace and bids you a safe return.

The Journey meditations are by Luna. Her article, "Air, Fire, Water, Earth & Spirit Power," appears on page 160.

SU	M	TU	W	TH	F	SA
						1
2	3	4	5	6	●	8
9	10	11	12	13	◑	15
16	17	18	19	20	○	22
23	24	25	26	27	28	◑
30	31					

March 9 • Daylight Saving Time begins, 2 am
March 16 • Palm Sunday
March 17 • St. Patrick's Day
March 20 • Ostara / Spring Equinox / International Astrology Day
March 21 • Purim / Good Friday
March 23 • Easter

ARIES

Journey for Fire

In a field outside of a wooded area on a dark, moonless night, the sky is brilliantly speckled with stars that light a faint trail in the woods ahead. The scent of pine rises to meet you and you enter the seemingly familiar forest as complete and utter peace and joy fills your heart. You see the outline of a small cottage in a clearing ahead and a light shining from behind a curtained window. You walk to the cottage, step onto a small front porch, and knock gently on the rough wooden door. Recognizing the scent of mulled cider and cinnamon, you feel welcome by the woman who stands before you. Her face is deeply lined with years of wisdom and understanding. She welcomes you with great love and compassion, and invites you to enter.

You step across the threshold, realizing that you are in the presence of the Crone. She beckons you to sit by the fire and warm yourself. Crackling logs and dancing flames bring the realization that this journey will reignite the flames in your life and this wise woman has something to reveal to you. She brings you a cup of warm cider and you join her by the fire as she reveals to you the secrets of Fire. The flame in her eyes warms your soul. Then, she leads you toward the door, away from the warmth of the fire in her cottage. She bids you a safe journey. With your skin newly warmed by the fire and your soul set ablaze from the spark of knowledge, you walk in the confidence of your journey, knowing that the Crone has gifted you the knowledge of Fire.

2008
APRIL

SU	M	TU	W	TH	F	SA
		1	2	3	4	●
6	7	8	9	10	11	◑
13	14	15	16	17	18	19
○	21	22	23	24	25	26
27	◑	29	30			

April 1 · All Fools' Day
April 20 · Passover begins
April 22 · Earth Day
April 25 · Orthodox Good Friday
April 27 · Orthodox Easter / Passover ends

TAURUS

Journey for Earth

Walking across a meadow, in a valley surrounded by mountains in the distance, you spot a worn pathway and begin to follow it toward the mountains. It's a beautiful spring day, the sky is full of the warming sun. The path you have chosen to walk diverges and you decide to take the path up to an opening in the rocks. As you walk up to the opening, you realize that it is a small cave and you feel a cool breeze from the depths of the mountain brush past to cool your sun-warmed face and neck. You look inside the cave and see that there is just enough light for you to explore the depths of the cave without any fear.

You walk just beyond the circle of light that is streaming into the cave and stop to allow your eyes to adjust. Using your hands to feel along the wall of the cave, you make your way along the wall, moving further away from the sunlit opening. A peaceful feeling washes over you. You walk deeper into the mountain and you see a stream of light pouring in from the ceiling of the cave. You walk toward the light and seat yourself in the center of the light. With your eyes closed, you lift your face up toward the light and allow it to wash over you. You feel the entire mountain enveloping you in its strong embrace. You sit in this circle of light, asking the mountain to reveal to you the secrets of Earth. As you accept the secrets of the mountain, you are thankful for this journey and you begin your descent back to the meadow carrying the Earth deep within your soul.

2008
MAY

SU	M	TU	W	TH	F	SA
				1	2	3
4	●	6	7	8	9	10
◑	12	13	14	15	16	17
18	○	20	21	22	23	24
25	26	◐	28	29	30	31

May 1 • Beltane
May 5 • Cinco de Mayo
May 11 • Mother's Day
May 26 • Memorial Day (observed)

GEMINI

Journey for Air

Walking along a beach as the brilliant shades of yellow and orange sink into the sea, the wind begins to blow and you seek shelter among the sand dunes. You feel the sea grasses whipping against your legs as you follow a path between the dunes. A faint glow emanates from inside the dunes and you walk toward it until you see a fire in the clearing. Standing by the fire is a tall man. He's starring into the flames and when you see him, there is immediate recognition. Warmth fills your heart as you embrace him and there is immediate peace and love. You sit by the fire-sheltered from the winds. From the distance comes the faint sounds of the crashing surf. The man's eyes are filled with compassion and wisdom, and they reflect the knowledge that a good life brings limitless rewards. His expression is one of deep and committed love. Slowly, he raises his chin and inhales deliberately, drawing in all of the air around you. The fire, once blazing, is now extinguished and you are sitting next to this great and wise Father. The full moon rising over the dunes offers the only light. Slowly, He exhales onto the logs and the fire is again burning brightly. He shares with you the secrets of Air.

As you stand and embrace this wise teacher, you know that He has shared more than a protective embrace with you. You walk out of the dunes assured that you will continue to discover the secrets of Air in your journey.

2008
JUNE

SU	M	TU	W	TH	F	SA
1	2	●	4	5	6	7
8	9	◐	11	12	13	14
15	16	17	○	19	20	21
22	23	24	25	◑	27	28
29	30					

June 9 · Shavuot
June 14 · Flag Day
June 15 · Father's Day
June 20 · Litha / Summer Solstice

CANCER

Journey for Spirit

You find yourself walking in a desert filled with beautiful red and orange rock formations. As you take in all of the beauty of your surroundings, the sky above you is darkening blue and seemingly endless. The vegetation awakens as the sun sinks behind the rocks. Knowing that you will need shelter before dark, you look for a place to settle in for the night, heading toward the rock formations. Up ahead, there is a grouping of trees and you can hear the sound of running water. As you approach, you also recognize the gentle melody of a flute and the faint sounds of a melodious feminine voice. You make your way toward the inviting sounds of water, music, and song, and see that there on the other side of the trees, are a young man and lady sitting by a small stream.

She wears a beautiful flowing dress and a wreath of flowers in her long auburn hair. Young and full of life, her lilting voice sings a song that was once familiar to you as she splashes in the water, singing and dancing. The young man plays a beautiful tune on the flute. He is young, strong, and virile, with long flowing black hair and a certain strong energy. They stop in their celebration and open their arms wide to embrace you. As they encircle you in their embrace you realize the meaning of Perfect Love and Perfect Trust in that instant. You are surrounded in complete protection and know that only that which is in your highest and best good will always prevail.

JULY

SU	M	TU	W	TH	F	SA
		I	●	3	4	5
6	7	8	9	◑	II	I2
I3	I4	I5	I6	I7	○	I9
20	2I	22	23	24	◑	26
27	28	29	30	3I		

July 4 · Independence Day

Lammas Harvest Spell

We have tilled the soil
And planted the seed.
Long did we toil
To get what we need.
The days now grow short,
The wheel, it has turned.
We sowed root and wort,
Now we reap what we've earned.
We harvest our fields,
Full of health, luck, and love,
We gather great yields
Of our gifts from above.
Prosperity grows
Even as the sun wanes.
Happiness glows
Though the late summer rains.
Our thanks overflowing,
Our hearts filled with glee,
We harvest our sowing,
Shouting, "So mote it be!"

Excerpt from Circle, Coven & Cove: A Year of Magickal Practice (Llewellyn, 2007) by Deborah Blake. Deborah's article, "Taking Their Leave," appears on page 208.

					2008 AUGUST	
SU	M	TU	W	TH	F	SA
					●	2
3	4	5	6	7	◐	9
10	11	12	13	14	15	○
17	18	19	20	21	22	◑
24	25	26	27	28	29	●
31						

August 1 · Lammas

Earthy Prosperity Tarot Spell

If possible, work this prosperity spell outdoors. You will be calling on the element of Earth. If weather permits, then set this up so your work area faces north.

Gather the following: a green votive candle; a votive-cup candle-holder; a half cup of garden soil (you can use potting soil); a saucer or small plate to hold the soil; the following tarot cards: Ace of Pentacles, Nine of Pentacles, and Ten of Pentacles (the suits of Coins and Pentacles are the same thing); a lighter or matches; and a safe, flat work surface to set up on.

Place the green votive candle inside the cup. Snuggle the votive cup securely into the soil. Arrange the cards next to the dish that holds the soil and candle. Center yourself. When you are ready, light the candle and speak the following spell three times:

Element of Earth I call, ground and strengthen me tonight.
May the gods now bless this green spell candle that burns so bright.
The suit of Pentacles and Coins calls for prosperity,
They will help to bring health and abundance quickly to me.

Close the spell by saying:

For the good of all, bringing harm to none,
By the element of Earth, this spell is done!

Allow the candle to burn out on its own. Remove the candle to a safe place, if necessary; never leave a burning candle unattended.

Excerpt from 7 Days of Magic (Llewellyn, 2004) by Ellen Dugan. Ellen's article, "Green Witchcraft," appears on page 88.

2008
SEPTEMBER

SU	M	TU	W	TH	F	SA
	1	2	3	4	5	6
◑	8	9	10	11	12	13
14	○	16	17	18	19	20
21	◐	23	24	25	26	27
28	●	30				

September 1 · Labor Day
September 2 · Ramadan begins
September 22 · Mabon / Fall Equinox
September 30 · Rosh Hashanah

Yoga Tree Posture

The depths of the soul can be reached only through quiet, soft moments. By exploring this depth, we learn about ourselves and where we fit within the web of existence that is life.

The yoga posture called "the tree" (*vrikshasana*) is about balance, and not just in the physical sense. I find that I have difficulty doing the tree pose if my energy is out of whack. When this occurs, I concentrate on calming myself first before trying the posture again because it aids in bringing me into balance. Because it requires physical balance, you have to put part of your mind into this function. Yoga is about the union of the body, mind, and spirit, and so to truly find balance in the tree pose, you have to reach inside yourself and bring your body, mind, and spirit into alignment.

To do the tree pose, stand up straight, but do not lock your knees. Place your hands on your hips and shift your weight to one foot. Think of your connection with the earth flowing through this foot as though you had roots. Bring the other foot up, with knee pointing to the side, to rest the sole on the inner thigh of the grounded leg. Rest; breathe slowly and steadily. When you are ready, bring your palms together in front of your chest, keeping your back straight and your body aligned. If you are comfortable with this, you can take this posture to its full extent by raising your hands above your head. Repeat the posture by balancing on the other leg.

Excerpt from Whispers from the Woods (Llewellyn, 2006) *by Sandra Kynes. Sandra's article, "The Zen Pagan Path," appears on page 64.*

2008
OCTOBER

SU	M	TU	W	TH	F	SA
			1	2	3	4
5	6	◑	8	9	10	11
12	13	○	15	16	17	18
19	20	◑	22	23	24	25
26	27	●	29	30	31	

October 2 · Ramadan ends
October 9 · Yom Kippur
October 13 · Columbus Day (observed)
October 14 · Sukkot begins
October 20 · Sukkot ends
October 31 · Samhain / Halloween

SCORPIO

Dark Moon in Scorpio

Water is a drop in Pisces, a stream in Cancer, and swells into a tidal wave in Scorpio. Scorpio is an extremely complex sign, full of intense emotions and actions. I think another symbol for Scorpio is the mermaid, with her beautiful head and torso above the surface and her powerful tail beneath the surface. Siren, as she was called, had a beautiful voice that made sailors abandon reason and steer their ships to the rocks. The mermaid chooses when she sings, where she swims, and whom she sees. Her mystery is revealed to only a few.

Tidal waves, like other great acts of nature, profoundly change things. The ocean floor is churned up and sea flora is moved to other places. New fish and animals repopulate the water. Tidal waves crash onto land and destroy the soil; they revitalize an area and prevent the soil from being depleted.

The intense power of nature frightens us. If we look beyond that fright, we know in an intuitive way that things like this happen for good reasons. In our brightly sunlit lives guided by the scientific method, we have been taught to know the facts and to understand what we learn from five of our senses. In the Dark Moon world, we can use our intuitive sense.

Excerpt from Rituals of the Dark Moon (Llewellyn, 2001) *by Gail Wood. Gail's article, "A Book of Shadows," appears on page 147.*

NOVEMBER

SU	M	TU	W	TH	F	SA
						1
2	3	4	◑	6	7	8
9	10	11	12	○	14	15
16	17	18	◐	20	21	22
23	24	25	26	●	28	29
30						

November 1 · All Saints' Day
November 2 · Daylight Saving Time ends, 2 am
November 4 · Election Day (general)
November 1 · Veterans Day
November 27 · Thanksgiving

A Winter Charm for the Home

Gather the following supplies:

- A small tube of iridescent glitter

- A basket (your choice of color and style)

- A square of felt (to line the basket)

- A dozen pinecones

Place the felt into the bottom of the basket. Arrange your pinecones in the basket. Hold your hands over the pinecones, and imagine the elements of Earth, Air, Fire, and Water swirling around you. Now picture this energy funneled down into your hands, and then sprinkle a bit of the glitter on top of the pinecones as you repeat this charm three times:

Pinecones are a natural symbol of fertility,
I enchant these to bring us good luck and prosperity.
By the winter winds that blow, and the sparkling snow that falls,
I call for joy and abundance to come bless us, one and all.

Place your basket on the hearth or use as a centerpiece this winter. Enjoy!

Excerpt taken from Cottage Witchery (Llewellyn, 2005) *by Ellen Dugan. Ellen's article "Green Witchcraft" appears on page 88.*

2008
DECEMBER

SU	M	TU	W	TH	F	SA
	1	2	3	4	◑	6
7	8	9	10	11	○	13
14	15	16	17	18	◐	20
21	22	23	24	25	26	●
28	29	30	31			

December 21 · Yule / Winter Solstice, December 22 · Hanukkah begins
December 24 · Christmas Eve, December 25 · Christmas Day
December 26 · Kwanzaa begins
December 29 · Hanukkah ends / Islamic New Year
December 31 · New Year's Eve

Group Workings

Early in my involvement in the magickal-spiritual community, I noticed a major problem in many public Craft circles: too much emphasis was placed on the framework of the ritual, rather than on the actual point of it. It's good (and necessary) to plan ahead and have a good idea of what is to be performed, who is going to perform it, and what traditional tools and ritualistic components will be used. One should not feel as though this procedure is immutable or unalterable. Witchcraft allows freedom to incorporate our own methodologies.

When entering a circle, we must be willing to completely surrender to the energy at hand and make the experience our own—for ourselves, for the group, and for the community and the world.

Ideally, every single participant should be involved in the circle so that the experience isn't empty or unfulfilling. Group rituals are tough because of the number of attendees, though it should be kept in mind that it's off-putting for people to be involved in bland or impersonal circles because of the lasting impressions they make on participant's spiritual quests.

Excerpt from Goth Craft (Llewellyn, 2007) *by Raven Digitalis. Raven's article "Who Decides that 'It' Is Only a Phase?" appears on page 50.*

2009
JANUARY

SU	M	TU	W	TH	F	SA
				1	2	3
◑	5	6	7	8	9	○
11	12	13	14	15	16	◐
18	19	20	21	22	23	24
25	●	27	28	29	30	31

January 1 · New Year's Day / Kwanzaa ends
January 19 · Birthday of Martin Luther King (observed)
January 20 · Inauguration Day
January 26 · Chinese New Year (ox)

Days of Power

Imbolc (February 2) marks the recovery of the Goddess after giving birth to the God. The lengthening periods of light awaken her. the God is a young, lusty boy, but his power is felt in the longer days. The warmth fertilizes the Earth (the Goddess), and causes seeds to germinate and sprout. And so the earliest beginnings of spring occur.

This is a sabbat of purification after the shut-in life of winter, through the renewing power of the sun. It is also a festival of light and of fertility, once marked in Europe with huge blazes, torches and fire in every form. Fire here represents our own illumination and inspiration as much as light and warmth.

Excerpt taken from Wicca: A Guide for the Solitary Practitioner *(Llewellyn, 1988) by Scott Cunningham.*

2009
FEBRUARY

SU	M	TU	W	TH	F	SA
1	◑	3	4	5	6	7
8	○	10	11	12	13	14
15	◐	17	18	19	20	21
22	23	●	25	26	27	28

February 2 · Imbolc / Groundhog Day
February 14 · Valentine's Day
February 16 · Presidents' Day (observed)
February 24 · Mardi Gras (Fat Tuesday)
February 25 · Ash Wednesday

Shamanism and Psychic Ability

Deepening psychic ability is a large part of shamanic and witch-craft training, another parallel of both arts showing that their roots are entwined. Shamans are known to give prophecy, speak with spirits to receive guidance, and "see things in the physical and nonphysical worlds that give them greater insight into the tribe's problems."

In shamanic traditions, the practitioner is encouraged to look at things in a nonordinary way to see nonordinary reality. By paying attention to what no one else looks at, and by doing what no one else does, the shaman can follow intuition and know what no one else knows. Many mystical traditions that have paralellels to shamanism encourage a nonordinary view of life (including ritual magick, alchemy, and yoga), but few spell it out as clearly as shamanic training.

The awareness that most people use is called First Attention. Most people in a community pay attention to the obvious. Very few look beyond the ordinary or expected. Observations are made on a surface level, and conclusions are drawn that are sometimes inaccurate.

Shamans cultivate Second Attention and are viewed as a bit peculiar with their new habits. They might stare off into space, immerse their attention in a pile of sand, or walk backwards. This might seem like "not doing," . . . but practitioners receive great benefits from not doing and just being.

Excerpt from The Temple of Shamanic Witchcraft: Shadows, Spirits, and the Healing Journey (*Llewellyn, 2005*) *by Christopher Penczak.*

2009
MARCH

SU	M	TU	W	TH	F	SA
1	2	3	◐	5	6	7
8	9	○	11	12	13	14
15	16	17	◐	19	20	21
22	23	24	25	●	27	28
29	30	31				

March 8 · Daylight Saving Time begins, 2 am
March 10 · Purim
March 17 · St. Patrick's Day
March 20 · Ostara / Spring Equinox / International Astrology Day

Moon Void-of-Course March 2008–March 2009

Last Aspect		New Sign	
Date	Time	Sign	New Time

MARCH 2008

Date	Time	Sign	New Time
1	11:54 am	1 ♑	1:33 pm
3	1:16 am	3 ♒	11:24 pm
5	4:46 pm	6 ♓	5:53 am
7	2:04 pm	8 ♈	9:23 am
10	7:09 am	10 ♉	12:13 pm
12	1:26 pm	12 ♊	1:54 pm
14	4:23 pm	14 ♋	4:37 pm
16	2:58 pm	16 ♌	9:04 pm
18	2:38 pm	19 ♍	3:25 am
20	3:28 pm	21 ♎	11:45 am
23	8:41 am	23 ♏	10:06 pm
25	8:36 pm	26 ♐	10:11 am
28	9:21 am	28 ♑	10:43 pm
31	12:54 am	31 ♒	9:34 am

APRIL

Date	Time	Sign	New Time
2	5:13 am	2 ♓	4:55 pm
4	5:43 pm	4 ♈	8:27 pm
6	11:01 am	6 ♉	9:19 pm
8	11:12 am	8 ♊	9:27 pm
10	12:11 pm	10 ♋	10:43 pm
12	2:32 pm	13 ♌	2:29 am
15	12:56 am	15 ♍	9:06 am
17	1:59 am	17 ♎	6:10 pm
19	4:54 pm	20 ♏	5:00 am
22	4:53 am	22 ♐	5:07 pm
24	5:37 pm	25 ♑	5:47 am
27	10:18 am	27 ♒	5:27 pm
30	1:25 am	30 ♓	2:11 am

MAY

Date	Time	Sign	New Time
2	5:34 am	2 ♈	6:51 am
4	3:16 am	4 ♉	7:58 am
6	4:21 am	6 ♊	7:17 am
7	9:36 pm	8 ♋	7:02 am
9	8:06 pm	10 ♌	9:10 am
12	4:09 am	12 ♍	2:48 pm
14	12:38 pm	14 ♎	11:46 pm
16	11:29 pm	17 ♏	10:59 am
19	10:11 pm	19 ♐	11:18 pm
22	12:19 am	22 ♑	11:55 am
24	8:26 am	24 ♒	11:51 pm
26	10:49 pm	27 ♓	9:38 am
29	2:23 am	29 ♈	3:52 pm
31	8:54 am	31 ♉	6:18 pm

JUNE

Date	Time	Sign	New Time
2	9:02 am	2 ♊	6:06 pm
4	8:08 am	4 ♋	5:16 pm
6	5:32 am	6 ♌	6:00 pm
8	11:40 am	8 ♍	10:01 pm
10	3:42 pm	11 ♎	5:55 am
13	5:15 am	13 ♏	4:53 pm
15	5:29 pm	16 ♐	5:19 am
18	5:37 pm	18 ♑	5:51 pm
20	3:02 pm	21 ♒	5:33 am
23	3:04 pm	23 ♓	3:32 pm
25	10:16 pm	25 ♈	10:49 pm
28	2:14 am	28 ♉	2:50 am
30	2:43 am	30 ♊	4:03 am

JULY

Date	Time	Sign	New Time
2	3:08 am	2 ♋	3:53 am
3	4:13 am	4 ♌	4:15 am
6	6:04 am	6 ♍	7:04 am
8	12:21 pm	8 ♎	1:31 pm
10	10:14 pm	10 ♏	11:35 pm
12	11:05 pm	13 ♐	11:50 am
15	10:44 pm	16 ♑	12:20 am
18	3:59 am	18 ♒	11:40 am
20	7:25 pm	20 ♓	9:07 pm
23	2:39 am	23 ♈	4:22 am
25	7:30 am	25 ♉	9:14 am
27	12:52 am	27 ♊	11:55 am
29	11:25 am	29 ♋	1:11 pm
31	1:31 am	31 ♌	2:21 pm

AUGUST

Date	Time	Sign	New Time
2	2:59 pm	2 ♍	4:59 pm
4	8:16 pm	4 ♎	10:28 pm
7	5:01 am	7 ♏	7:26 am
9	5:02 pm	9 ♐	7:10 pm
12	5:04 am	12 ♑	7:42 am
14	1:09 pm	14 ♒	6:56 pm
17	1:14 am	17 ♓	3:46 am
19	7:41 am	19 ♈	10:10 am
21	12:53 pm	21 ♉	2:38 pm
23	5:19 am	23 ♊	5:48 pm
25	5:52 pm	25 ♋	8:18 pm
27	8:13 pm	27 ♌	10:51 pm
29	11:44 pm	30 ♍	2:18 am

SEPTEMBER

Date	Time	Sign	New Time
1	5:01 am	1 ♎	7:44 am
3	1:09 pm	3 ♏	4:02 pm
5	11:45 am	6 ♐	3:11 am
8	12:43 pm	8 ♑	3:45 pm
10	9:15 am	11 ♒	3:19 am
13	9:19 am	13 ♓	12:04 pm
15	3:03 pm	15 ♈	5:39 pm
17	6:26 pm	17 ♉	8:56 pm
19	6:51 pm	19 ♊	11:17 pm
22	1:04 am	22 ♋	1:48 am
23	5:16 pm	24 ♌	5:13 am
26	7:20 am	26 ♍	9:52 am
28	1:31 pm	28 ♎	4:05 pm
30	9:47 pm	10/1 ♏	12:26 am

OCTOBER

Date	Time	Sign	New Time
9/30	9:47 pm	1 ♏	12:26 am
2	6:46 pm	3 ♐	11:14 am
5	9:08 pm	5 ♑	11:48 pm
7	3:37 pm	8 ♒	12:03 pm
10	7:13 pm	10 ♓	9:31 pm
13	1:02 am	13 ♈	3:07 am
15	3:36 am	15 ♉	5:31 am
17	3:33 am	17 ♊	6:25 am
19	5:52 am	19 ♋	7:40 am
21	7:54 am	21 ♌	10:35 am
23	1:53 pm	23 ♍	3:40 pm
25	9:02 pm	25 ♎	10:47 pm
28	6:05 am	28 ♏	7:47 am
30	1:45 am	30 ♐	6:41 pm

NOVEMBER

Date	Time	Sign	New Time
2	4:41 am	2 ♑	6:13 am
4	1:47 am	4 ♒	7:01 am
7	4:33 am	7 ♓	5:43 am
9	11:28 am	9 ♈	12:26 pm
11	2:17 pm	11 ♉	3:05 pm
13	12:12 pm	13 ♊	3:11 pm
15	2:17 pm	15 ♋	2:52 pm
17	8:43 am	17 ♌	4:07 pm
19	7:48 pm	19 ♍	8:12 pm
22	3:02 am	22 ♎	3:20 am
24	12:45 pm	24 ♏	12:54 pm
26	7:32 am	27 ♐	12:14 am
28	7:53 pm	29 ♑	12:48 pm

DECEMBER

Date	Time	Sign	New Time
1	10:44 am	2 ♒	1:44 am
3	9:14 pm	4 ♓	1:23 am
6	7:43 am	6 ♈	9:44 am
8	4:35 pm	9 ♉	1:52 am
10	5:23 pm	11 ♊	2:33 am
12	1:01 pm	13 ♋	1:39 am
14	5:27 pm	15 ♌	1:22 am
16	7:45 pm	17 ♍	3:35 am
19	5:29 am	19 ♎	9:23 am
21	11:57 am	21 ♏	6:36 pm
24	12:29 am	24 ♐	6:13 am
26	6:25 pm	26 ♑	6:56 pm
29	4:20 am	29 ♒	7:42 am
31	1:34 pm	31 ♓	7:27 pm

JANUARY 2009

Date	Time	Sign	New Time
3	3:50 am	3 ♈	4:50 am
4	9:44 pm	5 ♉	10:46 am
7	1:05 am	7 ♊	1:11 pm
9	1:39 am	9 ♋	1:14 pm
10	11:26 pm	11 ♌	12:41 pm
13	1:38 am	13 ♍	1:33 pm
15	9:37 am	15 ♎	5:30 pm
17	9:46 pm	18 ♏	1:20 am
19	10:36 pm	20 ♐	12:30 pm
22	11:23 am	23 ♑	1:18 am
25	4:08 am	25 ♒	1:56 pm
27	12:12 pm	28 ♓	1:12 am
30	4:23 am	30 ♈	10:25 am

FEBRUARY

Date	Time	Sign	New Time
1	1:08 pm	1 ♉	5:08 pm
3	8:27 pm	3 ♊	9:14 pm
5	12:44 pm	5 ♋	11:05 pm
7	2:07 pm	7 ♌	11:43 pm
9	2:28 pm	10 ♍	12:38 am
11	11:17 pm	12 ♎	3:33 am
14	9:46 am	14 ♏	9:50 am
16	4:37 pm	16 ♐	7:53 pm
18	8:36 pm	19 ♑	8:25 am
21	4:01 am	21 ♒	9:06 pm
23	9:08 pm	24 ♓	7:59 am
26	1:09 am	26 ♈	4:24 pm
28	12:51 pm	28 ♉	10:33 pm

MARCH

Date	Time	Sign	New Time
2	5:42 pm	3 ♊	2:59 am
4	9:10 pm	5 ♋	6:07 am
6	7:29 pm	7 ♌	8:24 am
9	3:56 am	9 ♍	11:34 am
11	1:48 pm	11 ♎	2:46 pm
13	6:39 pm	13 ♏	8:22 pm
15	8:43 pm	16 ♐	5:21 am
18	1:47 pm	18 ♑	5:18 pm
20	4:06 pm	21 ♒	6:06 am
23	8:09 am	23 ♓	5:08 pm
25	12:53 pm	26 ♈	1:03 am
27	10:17 pm	28 ♉	6:09 am
30	2:00 am	30 ♊	9:36 am

Eclipses (March 2008–March 2009)

Times are shown in Eastern Time

August 1, 6:22 am: Solar eclipse 9° ♌ 32'

August 16, 5:11 pm: Lunar eclipse 24° ♒ 21'

January 26, 1:58 am: 6° ♒ 30'

February 9, 8:38 am: 20° ♌ 59'

Full Moons (March 2008–March 2009)

Times are shown in Eastern Time

Storm Moon: March 21, 2:40 pm

Wind Moon: April 20, 6:25 am

Flower Moon: May 19, 10:11 pm

Strong Sun Moon: June 18, 1:30 pm

Blessing Moon: July 18, 3:59 am

Corn Moon: August 16, 5:16 pm

Harvest Moon: September 15, 5:13 am

Blood Moon: October 14, 4:02 am

Mourning Moon: November 13, 1:17 am

Long Nights Moon: December 12, 11:37 am

Cold Moon: January 10, 10:27 pm

Quickening Moon: February 9, 9:49 am

Storm Moon: March 10, 10:38 pm

Notes:

Notes:

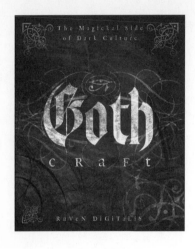

Goth Craft
THE MAGICKAL SIDE OF DARK CULTURE

Raven Digitalis

When paganism and gothic culture collide, a powerful blend of independent thought and magickal transformation is often the result. Raven Digitalis explores this dynamic intersection and what draws us to the "dark side."

Digitalis introduces many kinds of goths and witches, and the philosophy of each. Practical as well as insightful, *Goth Craft* covers the basics of magick, with special attention to blood magick, death magick, and necromancy. You'll also learn how to channel dark emotions, express yourself through the dark arts (clothes, hair, makeup, body modification), choose appropriate goth music for ritual, and myriad other ways to merge magickal practice with the goth lifestyle.

From working shadow magick to spellcasting on the dance floor, *Goth Craft* revels in the exciting convergence of two vital subcultures. Four pages of full-color photos, b/w photos. Call 1-877-NEW-WRLD to order this book.

978-0-7387-1104-1
7½ x 9⅛, 336 pp.
US $16.95
CAN $19.50

Goddess Alive!

INVITING CELTIC & NORSE GODDESSES INTO YOUR LIFE

Michelle Skye

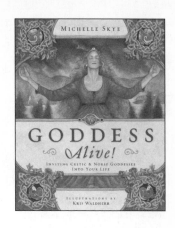

The seasons, moon phases, and even our personal experiences can be linked to the Divine Feminine. They have a face . . . they have a name . . . they have a goddess! Meet thirteen vibrant Celtic and Norse goddesses very much alive in today's world. Explore each deity's unique mythology and see how she relates to sabbats and moon rites. Lyrical meditations will guide you to otherworldly realms where you'll meet Danu, the Irish mother goddess of wisdom, and Freya, the Norse goddess of love and war. As you progress spiritually, you'll begin to see Aine in the greening of the trees and recognize Brigid in a seed's life-giving potential.

Goddess Alive! also includes crafts, invocation rituals, and other magical activities to help you connect with each goddess. Call 1-877-NEW-WRLD to order this book.

978-0-7387-1080-8
7½ x 9⅛, 288 pp.
US $18.95
CAN $20.95

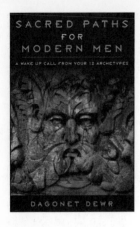

Sacred Paths for Modern Men

A WAKE UP CALL FROM YOUR 12 ARCHETYPES

Dagonet Dewr

Dagonet Dewr galvanizes the men's spirituality movement with this much-needed guide to divine masculinity. This book is not just for pagans, but for men of all faiths who want to explore and learn from their spiritual roots.

With humor and sensitivity, the author introduces twelve male archetypes—including the Child, the Warrior, the Lover, the Healer, and the Trickster—and the gods who embody them. Stories of deities from pagan lore and mythology spanning several cultures—and even characters from *The Lord of the Rings* and Arthurian literature—offer a rich framework for understanding the heritage of the sacred male. Rituals and magickal workings—for individual or group practice—offer practical ways to connect with these masculine energies and achieve a new understanding of their role in everyday life. Call 1-877-NEW-WRLD to order this book.

978-0-7387-1252-9
5³⁄₁₆ x 8, 264 pp.
US $14.95
CAN $16.95

Your Altar

CREATING A SACRED
SPACE FOR PRAYER AND
MEDITATION

Sandra Kynes

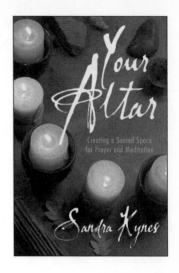

A reminder of the Divine, a space for spiritual encounter, or a focal point for meditation—the altar is a powerful tool for people of all faiths. Sandra Kynes demonstrates how to create personal altars and empower these sacred spaces according to your needs. Discover how to harness energies to manifest change, make decisions, receive wisdom, find balance, explore your soul, and grow spiritually. Kynes's unique approach provides nine overall matrices—each one corresponding to the number of objects placed on the altar—and the numerological significance of each. You'll also find suggested meditations and a wealth of helpful information—spanning chakras, colors, days of the week, elements, gemstones, gods/goddesses, runes, and more—for choosing appropriate symbols and objects that reflect your needs. Call 1-877-NEW-WRLD to order this book.

978-0-7387-1105-8
6 x 9, 240 pp.
US $15.95
CAN $18.50

Neopagan Rites

A GUIDE TO CREATING PUBLIC RITUALS THAT WORK

Isaac Bonewits

Isaac Bonewits pours over three decades of ritual experience—creating, attending, and leading ceremonies as a neopagan priest and magician—into this practical guide to effective ritual. Ideal for earth-centered spiritual movements and other liberal religious traditions, this book clarifies how to design powerful rites for small groups or large crowds.

Bonewits addresses every detail that contributes to successful public worship: the dynamics of participants, common worship patterns, the deities invoked, the risks of mixing spiritual traditions, pre-ritual preparation, and more. Learn to choose the optimal time, location, costume, props, and altar decorations. Enhance your ceremony with music, singing, poetry, dance, and movement. There are also invaluable tips for raising and channeling energy and using centers of power to send energy. Best of all, *Neopagan Rites* will help you create and perform rituals that unify, inspire, and fulfill their intended purpose. Call 1-877-NEW-WRLD to order this book.

978-0-7387-1199-7
6 x 9, 264 pp.
US $15.95
CAN $18.50

The Temple of Shamanic Witchcraft

SHADOWS, SPIRITS AND
THE HEALING JOURNEY

Christopher Penczak

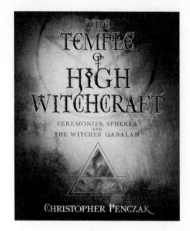

Is shamanism all that different from modern witchcraft?
According to Christopher Penc-
zak, Wicca's roots go back 20,000 years to the Stone Age shamanic traditions of tribal cultures worldwide. A fascinating exploration of the
Craft's shamanic origins, *The Temple of Shamanic Witchcraft* offers year-
and-a-day training in shamanic witchcraft.

Penczak's third volume of witchcraft teachings corresponds
to the water element—guiding the reader into this realm of emotion, reflection, and healing. The twelve formal lessons cover shamanic cosmologies, journeying, dreamwork, animal/plant/stone
medicine, totems, soul retrieval, and psychic surgery. Each lesson
includes exercises (using modern techniques and materials), as-
signments, and helpful tips. The training ends with a ritual for self-
initiation into the art of the shamanic witch—culminating in an act
of healing, rebirth, and transformation. Call 1-877-NEW-WRLD to
order this book.

978-0-7387-0767-8
480 pp., 7½ x 9½
US $17.95
CAN $24.50

Mystic Faerie Tarot

Artwork by
Linda Ravenscroft
Book by Barbara Moore

Step inside the enchanting world of the fey. Rich watercolor images by renowned artist Linda Ravenscroft capture the vibrancy and grace of faeries, sprites, elves, and nymphs in their lush gardens.

Each suit tells a "faerie tale" as the nature spirits embark on magical adventures. A water nymph and wood elf learn that love is a gift not to be taken lightly, while a foolish faerie queen and her kingdom are nearly overtaken by a magical blue rose. These stories offer lessons and fresh insights in all matters of life, while remaining true to tarot archetypes.

The Mystic Faerie Tarot kit includes a 288-page book that introduces tarot and describes the major and minor arcana in detail. Perfect for beginners, you'll also find faerie-themed spreads to use, along with sample readings and a quick reference guide to the cards. Boxed kit (5⅜ x 8¼) includes an 78-card deck, 312-page book, and an organdy bag with a satin cord. Call 1-877-NEW-WRLD to order.

978-0-7387-0921-5
US $24.95
CAN $27.50

Goddess Inspiration Oracle

Kris Waldherr

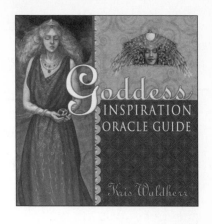

Draw strength from Diana, the beloved Roman huntress. Channel your anger wisely with help from the Hawaiian fire goddess Pele. Consult Anuket for prosperity. The Goddess Inspiration Oracle makes it easy for women to tap into the sacred wisdom of these powerful deities. Renowned for her superb goddess-themed artwork, Kris Waldherr has created a simple, visually stunning oracle deck for accessing the divine feminine. From Abeona to Zhinu, eighty goddesses from across the globe are represented in this classically ornate deck. Each card features a watercolor portrait of a deity, her attributes, and a message inspired by her unique story.

The enclosed guide offers in-depth descriptions of each goddess, keywords associated with her, and practical suggestions for working with the cards. Boxed kit (5³⁄₈ x 8¼) includes: 80-card deck, 120-pp. book, and a golden organdy bag. Call 1-877-NEW-WRLD to order.

978-0-7387-1167-6
US $21.95
CAN $25.50

The Well Worn Path

Raven Grimassi and Stephanie Taylor

Artwork by Mickie Mueller

Much more than a divination tool, *The Well Worn Path* is specifically designed for witches, Wiccans, and pagans. This uniquely pagan system is based on the roots of pagan culture and practice. Depicting symbolism and imagery vital to nature-based spirituality, the multifaceted, forty-card deck can be used for learning, teaching, ritual, and personal alignment. Each card has an assigned meaning, teaching element, and meditation for spiritual alignment that, altogether, communicates a vital pagan concept or tenet. It's a magical, transforming journey for students or teachers seeking to understand the hidden Mysteries and embrace the Old Ways. Boxed kit includes 40-card deck, 216-pp. book, and organdy bag. Call 1-877-NEW-WRLD to order this book. Call 1-877-NEW-WRLD to order.

978-0-7387-0671-9,
US $19.95
CAN $26.95

The Hidden Path

Raven Grimassi & Stephanie Taylor

Artwork by Mickie Mueller

Raven Grimassi and Stephanie Taylor introduce another innovative system exclusively for pagans, witches, and Wiccans.

Steeped in pagan tradition, practice and symbolism, *The Hidden Path* guides you to the tenets of this nature-based spirituality. Sensuous, vivid artwork captures the sabbats, the Fates, karma, centers of power, the Great Rite, and other pagan practices and beliefs still relevant today. Use this multi-faceted tool for celebrating seasonal rites, creating ritual experiences, pathworking, and accessing the hidden mysteries of the Craft. You'll also find a story woven throughout the deck for creating mystical alignments between you and the spiritual keys in the card imagery. The enclosed guidebook features interpretations and keywords for each card, divination spreads, and suggestions for incorporating the cards into your sabbat celebrations. Boxed kit (5³⁄₁₆ x 8¼) includes: 40-card deck, 216-pp. book, and a black bag. Call 1-877-NEW-WRLD to order.

978-0-7387-1070-9
US $19.95
CAN $22.95